MORE VIEWS FROM THE BOUNDARY
Volume One

One of the highlights of the BBC's *Test Match Special* is the Saturday lunchtime celebrity interview, 'Views from the Boundary', in which well-known personalities from all walks of life are invited into the commentary box by Brian Johnston to chat about themselves—and, of course, about cricket—over a glass of champagne. The guests may be writers, musicians, singers, jockeys, politicians or even weathermen. The only qualification they need for an invitation is a love of cricket. Brian Johnston's amiable but perceptive questioning has led to many memorable and fascinating conversations over the years and here are some of the best of them, from such varied characters as Max Jaffa, Michael Charlton, Eric Idle and Leslie Thomas.

MORE VIEWS FROM THE BOUNDARY

Volume One

Brian Johnston

Celebrity interviews from the
commentary box
Edited by Peter Baxter

CHIVERS LARGE PRINT
BATH

British Library Cataloguing in Publication Data available

This Large Print edition published by Chivers Press, Bath, 1994.

Published by arrangement with Methuen London, a division of Reed International Books.

U.K. Hardcover ISBN 0 7451 2235 3
U.K. Softcover ISBN 0 7451 2246 9

Line illustrations by Rodney Shackell

Photoset, printed and bound in Great Britain by
Redwood Books, Trowbridge, Wiltshire

CONTENTS

INTRODUCTION

Up to the end of the 1992 season we had invited seventy-five people to give *their* 'View from the Boundary'. It all started during the first Test against the West Indies at Trent Bridge in 1980, when dear old Ted Moult was our very first guest.

Three years ago the BBC published twenty of these Saturday lunchtime conversations in *Views from the Boundary*. Now another twenty-one are published in this collection called *More Views from the Boundary*.

These conversations—*not* interviews—are with well-known people who have a love of cricket, though they don't necessarily play it. We invite them to spend a Saturday of a Test Match in the commentary box with us on *Test Match Special*. We try to give them a little sustenance, usually a glass or two of champagne, reinforced by a tray lunch—airline style.

During the luncheon interval, after the news, we have about twenty-five minutes to talk. It is live, unscripted, uncensored(!) and with no prior knowledge of the questions. It is a most rewarding exercise to learn from such a variety of people something about themselves, and to find out just what cricket means to them and why they love it so.

In this new edition we certainly have a mixed variety of professions as proof that cricket is a link which knows no barriers of class, occupation nor background. In alphabetical order we offer you: an astronomer, an author, a Chancellor of the Exchequer, two comedians, a jazz pianist, a jockey, a political commentator, a violinist and a weather forecaster.

So now please join me in the commentary box. No champagne I'm afraid! But I do hope you enjoy yourself.

BRIAN JOHNSTON

MORE VIEWS FROM THE BOUNDARY

LESLIE THOMAS

Leslie is as hilarious in real life as are his characters in his many novels. I suppose he does sometimes stop talking but I have never experienced it! He is a very funny man with a tremendous knowledge of so many things. His time in the Army, his travels round the world, his spell as a writer on the *Evening News*, his collection of antiques and of course, after a late start, his love of cricket. He worships cricketers and enjoys nothing better than playing cricket alongside old England players for the Lord's Taverners. He may not be a great cricketer but he takes it very seriously, and tries like mad. In September 1992 I was umpiring in a Taverners' Charity Match on a lovely little school ground in the Close at Salisbury, where Leslie now lives. He caught a sizzling catch at deep mid-wicket, made it look very easy and tossed the ball up in the air like a true professional. I'm glad to say—though perhaps *he* was disappointed—that the Taverners did *not* rush up and kiss him!

He is a permanently busy man. When he joined us at the Oval in 1981 he had come up especially from Somerset and was off the next day to play cricket at Arundel. He had just returned from travels abroad, was preparing to launch his fiftieth novel, *The Magic Army*, in October and had already begun yet another book, *A World of Islands*. I started by asking him how much he enjoyed his travelling all round the world.

THE OVAL, 29 AUGUST 1981

LESLIE THOMAS The trouble is, going to these places abroad you miss the cricket and I have to try to find you on the overseas service and all I get is the Top Forty—whatever that may be.

BRIAN JOHNSTON Were all those novels on the Army based on your actual experiences when you were in the Army?

LESLIE Yes. My entry in *Who's Who* says, 'rose to the rank of lance corporal', which is all I ever did.

BRIAN Were you stationed abroad?

LESLIE Yes, in Singapore, where we played cricket. I remember getting off a plane in Singapore once and asking the taxi driver to take me to the Padang, where they played cricket, and I sat under the same tree where I sat as a soldier when I was eighteen years old and watched cricket—and I swear it was the same two batsmen still in.

BRIAN   When did cricket start in your life, then?

LESLIE   Well, I never told anyone this, Brian, but very late. I was telling my son last night that at the age of twelve I didn't know how many men were in a cricket team.

BRIAN   Oooh—sacrilege!

LESLIE   I know, it's a terrible thing to say, but I was brought up in wartime in Newport, Mon., which was not a centre of cricket, despite what Wilfred Wooller told me recently, that they did play matches there, and I honestly didn't know anything about the game until I went to live in Devon—and it was March and I was batting in the nets and another batsman got behind me because I was missing so many of the balls.

BRIAN   Where was this in Devon?

LESLIE   In Kingsbridge.

BRIAN   Very nice—on the river down there.

LESLIE   Yes, in fact my novel, *The Magic Army*, is set at that period during the War in Devon. It's about the huge invasion army waiting to invade Europe.

BRIAN   And did you develop into a batsman in the end?

LESLIE   No, I never did. Actually, this is a fraud. I've played cricket all my life and frankly I've never been much good, except I've always been very enthusiastic. I love the game. I love playing it, watching it, reading about it—everything about it. When I was in my teens, if I made a duck on a Sunday I couldn't sleep the whole week and it made me miserable, but now, you see, I go out for the fun and strangely enough I do get some runs. I've had a couple of fifties and I made ten not out for Prince Charles' XI.

BRIAN Not on a horse.

LESLIE Well, almost. It was on the polo ground at Windsor—the first time cricket had ever been played there.

I was playing golf yesterday with a great friend called Ben and he's very tough and he thinks cricket's a poof's game and he told me so. So I said I'd send Lillee round to see him and he said, 'There, I told you—Lily.'

BRIAN Are you any good at golf?

LESLIE So-so. I played with Peter Alliss on television a couple of years ago and I did reasonably well. I think that some days I play like Arnold Palmer and some days like Lili Palmer.

BRIAN You did that *A Round With Alliss*. How many holes did you get through?

LESLIE Oh, about five. I had a two on one hole, it was terrific. But I think he's a tremendous man.

BRIAN What about cricket, though. Have you supported Glamorgan?

LESLIE Do you know, I've just been asked to write a chapter for a book that's coming out next year in which each chapter is about a different county and I'm writing about

4

Glamorgan—about the daffodil summer, the summer they won the championship. I went to see Wilfred Wooller the other day, had lunch with him and he was terrific. I'd never met him before. I love cricketers, you know. Sir Leonard Hutton is a great friend of mine, because I used to write a column for him when I was on a newspaper. I saw him at Lord's the other day and I'm always so pleased to see him and I think it's mutual; we really like each other.

BRIAN   You wrote his cricket column for him?

LESLIE   Years ago, yes. I was on the *Evening News* and it was headed 'SIR LEONARD HUTTON SAYS' and underneath in very small type 'as told to Leslie Thomas'. But I didn't mind, it was a great privilege.

BRIAN   Did you learn a lot from him?

LESLIE   Tremendous, yes. Terrific sense of humour. He's a singular man. Some people think he's a very hard man, but he isn't. He's one of the most interesting men I've ever met. We were at Worcester and on the first day I bought lunch. On the second day he bought lunch—he was getting about fifty thousand quid more than me—and on the third day he brought sandwiches. I'd got a little packet of crisps and he said, 'Those crisps look OK.' So I said, 'Well, help yourself.' And he delved into the crisps, ate a handful and then said, 'They're better with

5

salt.' So I said, 'There's some salt there somewhere.' He had some more and by the time he'd finished there were three crisps in the bottom of the packet. So I said, 'Well, you might as well eat them all now.' And he said, 'No, lad, you eat them. They're your crisps.'

(Sir Leonard Hutton died in September 1990 at the age of 74. Ed.)

BRIAN You say you didn't know about cricket till you were twelve. Who did you watch? Who were your heroes?

LESLIE Oh, R. S. Ellis of Australia in the Australian Services team in 1945. Spin bowler. I modelled my bowling on R. S. Ellis. A blank look's come on your face. R. S. Ellis—same team as Cristofani and Miller. The first cricketer I ever saw, in fact, was Keith Miller—at the Leyland Ground at Kingston-on-Thames. He was reading a sporting paper and I asked for his autograph and he said, 'Have you got anything good for the four-thirty?'

BRIAN That's typical Miller.

LESLIE You know, to sit up here today is absolutely wonderful for me. It's so cosy, isn't it? And you get drinks and eats.

BRIAN But you kept so quiet there.

LESLIE Well, I did for once in my life, because I was fascinated. You can actually see the ball moving and I know that all this stuff you do on the radio is absolutely true.

I live in Somerset now, where they're all cricket barmy—men, women and children—and when Botham was making his runs at Headingley, we had a house full of workmen and one got so excited he fell down the ladder.

(This conversation took place six weeks after the famous Headingley Test of 1981, when Ian Botham's innings of 149 not out enabled England to beat Australia by 18 runs after following on 227 behind. Ed.)

BRIAN Why have you gone to Somerset?

LESLIE My son's going to Millfield. That's the sum total of it. And we want him to go as a day boy. I want him to be able to spell. I think he'll have a wonderful time there.

BRIAN Can you spell?

LESLIE I'm not bad. I always think spelling is something you can get from a book. People say to me, 'Who actually writes your books? Do they put the full stops in?' Because they think I couldn't possibly do it.

BRIAN Can you listen to Test Match commentary going on as you write, or do you have to shut yourself away?

LESLIE I sneak off every now and then and turn the television or the radio on.

Something happened to me last year which I just couldn't believe. I went to the Centenary Test Match Dinner and I was sitting next to Bobby Simpson and I went out for something or other and when I came

7

back he said, 'There's a young man over there would like your autograph.' So I said, 'Why didn't he ask?' He said, 'Oh, he's very shy.' So I signed the autograph and asked, 'Who is it for?' He said, 'That chap over there, Kim Hughes.' I thought, my God, I should ask for his autograph.

(At this time Kim Hughes was the Australian captain. Ed.)

BRIAN   Have you ever thought of writing a book with cricket as a background to it?

LESLIE   No. Cricket does tend to creep into a lot of my books. *The Magic Army*, which I've just finished—it's a very long novel, about a quarter of a million words—as the armies go off to invade Europe, there's a village cricket match taking place. I checked the local papers down there and on 6 June there was a cricket match. There's the story of a titled lady who was absolutely shocked as she was coming back from Dover at the time of Dunkirk with troops and wounded and everything on her train and as they went past Wimbledon there were fields full of cricketers in white.

BRIAN   It all goes back to Sir Francis Drake. 'The Armada can wait; my bowels can't.' Isn't that what he said?

LESLIE   Is that what he said?

BRIAN   They said he was playing bowls, but he had to rush off when he saw the Armada coming. But your book—a quarter of a million words!

LESLIE It took three years.

BRIAN Do you do a wadge and then sort of correct?

LESLIE I do about a thousand words a day. In fact the BBC have done a television documentary about the writing of this book. It's in three parts. They followed me around and they filmed the writing and the research and all that sort of thing.

BRIAN Do you keep yourself to a thousand words a day or do you do as many as you feel you can that day?

LESLIE The worst mornings I sit there—just as you have to come here when there's no play and it's raining—and I put my hands on that typewriter and I write a thousand words whatever. That's being professional, I think.

BRIAN Yes, it is, but supposing you don't get that inspiration.

LESLIE Oddly enough, the morning you don't get the inspiration, if you just press on and press on, it's frequently the best morning that you have.

BRIAN You get these marvellous comic scenes. If they're not taken from life, how do you conjure them up?

LESLIE Well, a lot of them are taken from life, because life's very funny, I think. If you look at it from a certain angle and see the amusing things—even in the most dreadful tragedy. I saw the most grotesque thing in Spain. We were having dinner in an open-air restaurant by a road that was just like a killer track. There were accidents all the time along this stretch of road and there was the most frightful crash just below us. There was a man in the restaurant playing one of these little organs and he switched to the Dead March. There were people lying about everywhere, but that's the sort of grotesque humour that does happen in life.

BRIAN What about your time in Fleet Street?

LESLIE I worked on the *Evening News* when it sold a million and a half copies a night—no thanks to me—but it was a great newspaper then and I had a wonderful life. I went to about eighty countries. I travelled with the Queen and the Duke of Edinburgh and I went all over the world. In fact, when I wrote my first novel, *The Virgin Soldiers*, and it became a best-seller, it was a double-edged thing, because it meant I had to leave Fleet Street and in fact I went back and got an office in Fleet Street, because it was home. Now I only miss Fleet Street at lunchtime.

BRIAN One of the things they say you're interested in is antiques. Is that so?

LESLIE Yes. My wife had an antique business for some years and we have a sort of collection of bits and pieces. We had a stall in Portobello Road at one time. It was great

10

fun. People used to come down and see me standing there in the morning and think, 'Oh he's down on his luck, poor fellow.' I used to go and buy bits of china and if we made ten pounds at the end of the day or twenty pounds—this is some years ago—we were so happy. More than all the royalties. I suppose it's ready money.

BRIAN Now what about the winter? You wouldn't be tempted to follow a team round on tour?

LESLIE No, I've seen relatively little cricket abroad, strangely enough. I saw a Test Match once in Trinidad. I came straight off the boat, went to the day's play in the Test Match and got straight on the boat again and went away. It was when Cowdrey made a big score.

BRIAN Well, you're going to watch the rest of the day with us, I hope.

LESLIE You bet. This is where I'd like to come every time I come to the Oval.

MICHAEL CHARLTON

Michael Charlton was unusual. He was an Australian cricket commentator with a 'Pommie' accent during the 1950s. He also introduced the Australian equivalent of BBC TV's *Panorama* called *Window on the World*. Sadly—for us—he deserted cricket to become a political commentator and interviewer full time, coming over to work in England, where he still lives. He was a splendid contrast to the normal Australian cricket commentator, with a delightful sense of humour portrayed with a friendly chuckle. He was the ABC commentator over here in 1956 and we started my conversation with him with a clip from his own commentary during the Old Trafford Test in 1956—Laker's match. He described a unique wicket—Burke caught Cowdrey bowled Lock 22. It was unique because it was the only wicket Tony Lock took during the match, Jim Laker taking the other nineteen.

HEADINGLEY, 14 JULY 1984

MICHAEL CHARLTON It was remarkable, wasn't it. Two world-class spinners, one of whom gets nineteen wickets and the other gets only one.

BRIAN JOHNSTON Tony Lock's still trying to work it out. Laker got all his wickets from the same end—the Stretford End. Locky bowled from that end as well.

MICHAEL Yes, so it was the same for both. I remember going out to the wicket when it was all over and what I shall never forget is a small circle on a length on off stump in which it looked as if a whole series of two shilling pieces had been put down—and that was Laker. He'd bowled absolutely on this spot. I thought he was just about unplayable.

BRIAN Well, now, travelling round with the team you get to know all their feelings and inner secrets. Publicly they said the pitch was made to measure for Laker, although in fact England made 459 on it.

MICHAEL It was the same for both sides, wasn't it? There was a lot of controversy about that pitch. I think the Australians thought they'd been taken for a ride. They thought that that pitch at Old Trafford that time was not the traditional one. Some new soil had been put on it and all that kind of thing, but it was the same for both sides. Not a happy tour all round, I think, that one for

13

the Australians. They were on a down-swing that time. I think also that they weren't as well led as they might have been and I think there was a general feeling—certainly my own feeling—that Keith Miller should have captained that side.

BRIAN Let's just remind people that the first Test of that 1956 series was drawn at Trent Bridge and then the second one at Lord's Australia won.

MICHAEL Yes, Miller won that. Extraordinary figure he was. I remember him as he came off the field throwing a bail to somebody.

BRIAN There's a picture of him, it's been captured and I've seen it in books.

MICHAEL He had a flair for that, didn't he? *(Miller took ten wickets in the Lord's Test. Ed.)*

BRIAN Then England won the third Test by an innings here at Headingley and then they won the Old Trafford one by an innings and the fifth was drawn.

Let's talk about Miller for a second, because you say he should have been captain. How good a captain do you reckon he was?

MICHAEL Well he was a very fine captain of the state side of New South Wales, because I think he was an inspirational captain. He was not a man to speak coherently and explain things in detail before matches began. He wasn't that kind of player, I think we all

14

know. But he could inspire great loyalty in a side and I think that young side in New South Wales absolutely worshipped him. He could do as he liked and he had great luck of course. I think whatever it was Horatio said about Hamlet, had he been put on he was likely to have proved most royal. He was a most inspiring figure.

BRIAN But he had this lovely, casual approach in everything he did.

MICHAEL Jimmy Burke, who died so tragically, told me of a match we were all at at Newcastle. It must have been a country match and Miller was captain of the New South Wales side and they walked out in the morning under rather a hot sun. Miller's eyes were shielded against the sun this particular morning and Burke said to him, 'Excuse me, Nugget (they all called him Nugget), there are twelve men.' And Miller, without turning round, said, 'Well somebody bugger off, then.' And just kept on—didn't even look round.

BRIAN Jimmy Burke was a great character. He became a very good commentator, didn't he?

MICHAEL Well, that was long after my time. He was a wonderful tourist, a great mimic, a very amusing boy. He was a happy character when I knew him.

BRIAN And he could imitate somebody throwing when he bowled.

15

MICHAEL Yes, he had the most dreadful action.

BRIAN I don't think people minded much because it wasn't very effective.

(J. W. Burke, who played 24 Tests for Australia between 1950 and 1958, committed suicide at the age of 49 in 1979. Ed.)

BRIAN What actually was your period of commentating? We knew you in 1956, when you came here.

MICHAEL Round about '52 I was doing Sheffield Shield matches and then I did the '54 tour, England's tour of Australia—Len Hutton's tour. Then there were some in India.

BRIAN You were there in 1958/59, my first time when I came out to Australia.

MICHAEL Yes, I remember you getting bowled over in the surf at Bondi and Jack Fingleton laughing.

BRIAN Yes, someone shouted, 'There's one out the back,' or something. What's it called? I was 'dumped'.

MICHAEL You were dumped, yes. I remember you striding heroically into the surf and appearing like a torpedo about five minutes later, belching sand and salt water.

BRIAN You were a bit extraordinary to be a commentator in Australia, because you had what they used to describe as a slightly Pommie voice.

MICHAEL It's always difficult to explain,

but my parents were New Zealanders and we were always brought up very strictly at home not to speak the colonial twang, as my father called it. So it's an environmental thing, largely, coming from my father. We always called England 'home'. In fact, when I came here in '56, they wanted me to sound more Australian. They were a bit disturbed by that.

BRIAN But you were a bit different. The average Australian commentator is not quite as light-hearted as we are and certainly you were light-hearted. You saw the fun in it.

MICHAEL Too often, perhaps. Yes, I always looked for that myself. I think it's the most marvellous witty and amusing game. We were brought up, of course, in the Bradman era and they always said about him that he'd be trying to get a hundred against the blind school. It was a serious business in Australia. I think Don Bradman's seriousness of purpose rather overlaid it, you know. It sat upon its soul like a mountain for many years.

BRIAN Why did you give all this up, then, because you obviously love cricket so much?

MICHAEL Well, I very much ask myself that. The best years I had were undoubtedly going round the world with cricketers and cricket teams. I loved it and I felt quite tearful coming back here this morning. I haven't been here, to this ground, for twenty-eight years. I had the most

17

marvellous time. I suppose because of the rather puritan background, I wondered, at the age I was—mid-twenties—if one was going to go on doing this for the rest of one's life. Oddly enough, it was through cricket that my life was pretty much changed to politics because I was in Delhi once, doing a Test Match there on the Australian tour—Richie Benaud's tour—and I sat next to Nehru, the Prime Minister of India. And I interviewed him on the strength of this later and I got a bit of a taste for this and I ended up doing that ever after.

BRIAN   Why did you decide to come over here? We're very glad you did.

MICHAEL   I was invited, Johnno. They asked me to come and I've been here ever since.

BRIAN   I want to take you back now to perhaps one of the most exciting matches you ever did. The tie in 1960 at Brisbane.

MICHAEL   I brought my tie to show you. Specially for you I wear it.

BRIAN   That's the famous tie. Is it everyone who was there who can wear it?

MICHAEL Any one of the players or correspondents who were there can wear it. It's a rather unimaginative thing, as you see. It's the West Indies colours and the gold and green.

BRIAN   What's this insignia?

MICHAEL   Well, you might well ask. Fingo designed this—Jack Fingleton—and it's a golden tied knot. It's the tie for what must be—I don't know, a lot of water's gone down many rivers since then—the greatest Test Match ever played.

BRIAN   I think it must have been. And yet the strange thing is, we hear very strange stories of how—it wasn't you—but one of the Australian commentators who was on at the end, didn't realise what the result was and I think said it was a draw and the next day had to go back and do a cod commentary for the archives with some people applauding in the box.

MICHAEL   Well, I've not heard that. We all left the ground in the dawn next morning. Nobody went to bed that night—players, public or the travelling press. There was confusion at the end. It was the last over, last day and the last couple of balls of the Test Match and you know those huge tropical sunsets in the north in Australia—it was like a scarlet ribbon. It was quite hard to see the scoreboard. And the scoreboard panicked, because of all these run-outs at the end, because you very nearly had completed runs. Everybody had their hands on the trigger. Everybody was saying, 'It's all over. They've won.' And it wasn't won, because all these hairline decisions for run-outs were being given. I'd done the commentary period just before the Test Match ended, the penultimate twenty minutes. Clive Harburg

19

did the last session and I was down on the
field just as they came off and Joe Solomon
thought the West Indies had won and
Worrell, the captain, thought they'd lost. It
was quite confusing. The ABC scorer kept
his head. He was marvellous. He had it right.
BRIAN No names, no pack drill, but certain
well-known commentators and ex-Test
cricketers writing for newspapers had left the
ground and heard the result when they
arrived by air in Sydney.
MICHAEL They had indeed. There were
those—and we dare not speak their names,
even now—who left before the last hour or
so, assuming that Australia were going to
win. It would have been a remarkable Test
Match even if it hadn't had the finish that it
did. There was a wonderful innings by a
glamorous young Australian in the first
innings—O'Neill made 181. There was an
absolutely superb innings by Sobers—132.
And there were two shots in that innings in
particular. He hit something through
mid-wicket—a pull shot, but the trajectory of
that shot I can still see. It never rose more
than about five feet above the ground. I
thought it must have been like that at
Trafalgar on Nelson's ships, with a
cannonball carrying away the rigging. It went
straight over the fence like a rocket and it
mowed down the crowd. Then he hit
something that hit Colin McDonald at very

deep mid-off on the shoulder. An off-drive off Benaud, I think, and it hit McDonald on the left shoulder as he put a knee down to field it and it hit the sight board. That was Sobers. Anyway, it all came down to this. Australia had to get 233 to win in 300 minutes and it looked as if they would do it easily.

(A seventh wicket stand between Benaud and Davidson had taken them from 92 for 6 to 226 for 7. Ed.)

And it got down to this last over at four minutes to six, I remember, in this blood-red sunset and almost hysterical excitement. Australia had to get six runs off eight balls and there were three wickets to fall and Benaud had batted marvellously throughout the afternoon. I was talking to Richie, whom I hadn't seen for years, only this morning and he said that Frank Worrell went over to Wes Hall, who was to bowl this last over, and said, 'No bouncers, Wes.' So the first thing Wes Hall did was to bowl a bouncer and Benaud hooked it—and I have Richie's authority to say this—he said it should have been six, but he got a top edge and it went miles high and Alexander, the wicket keeper, caught it marvellously over his head.

(Benaud out for 52—five runs needed to win off six balls. The new batsman, Meckiff, was nearly run out taking a bye off his second ball. Four were needed off four balls. Ed.)

Wally Grout hooked the next one from Hall—skied it to mid-wicket. Now, Wes Hall was soaked with sweat. He was bowling like a hurricane and his shirt was flapping all over the place. I remember the umpires kept having to stop him and tell him to tuck his shirt in, because this billowing sail, this spinnaker, was obscuring everybody's view. The umpire couldn't see. Anyway, Wally Grout skied this to Rohan Kanhai at mid-wicket and Kanhai had all day and all night to get underneath this, except that Hall, who was doing all his own fielding, changed course and I swear he was doing fifty miles an hour. He galloped across and he barrelled into Kanhai, knocked him flying and it went to ground. They got a single. Three were needed off three balls. The four thousand people who saw this are the members of the most exclusive and boring club in the world.

BRIAN I've never heard it in such detail.

MICHAEL So Meckiff let fly at the next ball from Wes Hall and he hooked him far out to deep mid-wicket, on the far mid-wicket fence and again you could hardly see in this terrific sunset.

BRIAN A four would have won the match.

MICHAEL Of course. And they rushed off. They took the first two. Wally Grout turned for the third and Conrad Hunte—he was a beautiful player, Hunte—he threw. It must

22

have been the throw of a lifetime. He was travelling round the boundary, right on the boundary line. He scooped it up and he threw it over the top of the stumps and Grout was flying for these last few yards. He hurled himself along the ground. He skidded on his stomach—out by half a foot, something like that. He got up covered in red dust and people were hysterical by this time. Kline came in and he hit the first one to forward short leg and Joe Solomon threw Meckiff out from side on. And so there was this enormous confusion, you see, with people running around. I think the official attendance that day was four thousand and I shall never forget, like Colonel Maitland at Waterloo—you must know this, Johnno, as a guardsman—'Stand up, Guards!', that crowd stood up as one man and they came over that fence like a wall and they rushed the pavilion. Frankie Worrell came off and I remember him saying, 'Man, this is a game for cool fools.' And Bradman, who was below us, he had a newspaper in his hands and the thing was in tatters, it was twisted so much. Like a stage magician with a torn paper act.

BRIAN And the celebrations that night.

MICHAEL The West Indians sang calypsos all night. The crowds were out in the streets. I've never seen anything like it.

BRIAN Well, happy memories and how

could you really have left that for a world of interviewing kings and prime ministers? Is it fun?

MICHAEL   Well, yes it is, but it's a different kind of amusement.

BRIAN   Do you get a few laughs?

MICHAEL   I wouldn't say there are many laughs, no. I would say it's a fairly detached sort of amusement. It's not the generous, carefree, likeable world that you all happily reflect here.

LESLIE CROWTHER

Sadly on 3 October 1992 Leslie had a horrendous car accident. His Rolls Royce veered off a motorway into the embankment on the side of the road. It turned completely over, with Leslie still inside. Miraculously—thanks no doubt to the solid bodywork of the Rolls—he was able to get out and, still conscious, was even able to crack jokes with his rescuers. However, after being taken to hospital, he had a severe relapse and went into a coma which was to last for six weeks. He was transferred to Frenchay Hospital in Bristol where he underwent two operations on his brain. At first, when he came out of his coma, due to tracheotomy he was unable to speak, but could write things down. There are two delightful stories about this. His wife Jean opened a letter addressed to him from No. 10 Downing Street asking if he would agree to accept the award of a CBE. She whispered into his ear that he *must* sign his acceptance and it was the very first thing he wrote. On another occasion one of his daughters was exercising his brain by asking him to identify and point at various shapes—circles, squares etc. She felt he was not concentrating so reprimanded him gently and said, 'Come on, Dad, concentrate, and try harder.' He immediately reached for his pencil and paper and hastily scribbled just one word: 'Bollocks'. Recovery was under way! As I write Leslie is back home and making steady progress.

I suppose a lot of people think of Leslie as a presenter of *Crackerjack* and his famous 'come on down' in the quiz show *The Price is Right*. But of course he is far more than that. He is one of the top five stand-up comedians in the country, performing in cabaret, pantomime and especially as an after-dinner speaker. He has a fund of stories and jokes, usually topical, and is a great ad-libber with any interrupters.

Besides his work he is a tremendous worker for charity. In 1991 and 1992 he was President of the Lord's Taverners for whom he made nearly 350 appearances at various events, every one requiring a speech from him.

When he joined us in the box at Old Trafford in 1985 it was a wet day. So we had a rather longer session than usual during 'Rain Stopped Play', though he had to leave us in mid-afternoon to go back to Blackpool where he was appearing twice nightly in *The Price is Right*. I mentioned his quick wit as an ad-libber. You will find proof of this with his final remark of our conversation!

OLD TRAFFORD, 3 AUGUST 1985

BRIAN JOHNSTON I got you to sign something just now and you did it with your left hand. Are you a left-hander at cricket?

LESLIE CROWTHER I'm a left-handed bowler. Fred Trueman, who is godfather to our son, Nicholas, describes my bowling as left arm blankety blank over the wicket, which is very accurate. But I bat right-handed.

BRIAN So where did you start your cricket? When did you first become interested in it?

LESLIE I first became interested at the Scarborough Festival when I was in a show called the Fol-de-Rols, which was a concert party, as you know. The Australians were playing and Neil Harvey was over and so were Keith Miller and Ray Lindwall and all that lot.

BRIAN Sounds like '53.

LESLIE That's right, it was. I went along and I suddenly saw all these magical people in real life, as it were, and I became totally besotted and I've followed cricket ever since.

BRIAN Did you play at school?

LESLIE I did, but I was very bad. I wasn't

27

any good at any kind of sports. I had a very strange illness called meningitis.

BRIAN You were lucky to get away with it.

LESLIE In the late forties I was very lucky to get away with it. They diagnosed it as scarlet fever and I was shoved in a scarlet fever ward, so I had to be cured of scarlet fever before they could start on the other.

BRIAN You wear glasses, so that would have affected your cricket—the fact that you're short-sighted.

LESLIE Oh, very short-sighted, yes, but nothing affects my cricket. It's always been bad.

BRIAN So when you started in 1953, which team did you take up as your favourite?

LESLIE England. I thought that was a good team to take up. I didn't bother with a county, just went straight for the country. Lately, of course, I've been following the fortunes of Somerset, because that's where we've moved and it seems a fairly good team with people like Richards and Garner and another chap called Botham.

BRIAN You're near sunny Bath, are you?

LESLIE Yes, about three miles. The Bath cricket festival, of course, is great, now they've sorted out that wicket.

BRIAN It's lovely, isn't it? So who were your heroes after 1953 in the English cricket scene?

LESLIE Oh, Peter May, Ted Dexter, Tom

28

Graveney, Ken Barrington—the really elegant strokemakers. You were saying earlier that cricket and the theatre are very aligned and that there is something in common with the two professions and there is. The thing about cricket, although some people call it a slow game, it's a very very dramatic game and every player gets his entrance and his exit—very often sooner than he wants to—but it's a dramatic game and I love it.

BRIAN There is this affinity and it's partly because cricketers enjoy meeting people from the stage.

LESLIE That's right. When I was in a thing called *Let Sleeping Wives Lie* at the Garrick Theatre, there was a nervous tap on the dressing room door one evening and Johnny Gleeson was ushered in. And apparently, when he came to England to play in that marvellous series with that incredible bowling that nobody could fathom, he went to every single West End show and introduced himself shyly to everybody.

(J. W. Gleeson toured England in 1968 and 1972 and played in 29 Tests for Australia, bowling an enigmatic mix of off–and leg-breaks. Ed.)

BRIAN Back in Australia he was a farmer and used to have to go 120 miles each Saturday to play in his game and he didn't see any theatre. I remember talking to him about it and he literally went to everything when he came here.

LESLIE   He absolutely adored it and so we got to know him very well. There was a wonderful moment in *Let Sleeping Wives Lie* with Brian Rix, who, as you know, is potty about the game, Leo Franklyn—wonderful chap, mad about cricket—and myself and Bill Treacher and there was a Test in the West Indies when all England had to do was draw the last match to win the series.

BRIAN   That was Colin Cowdrey's tour in 1968. Jeff Jones came in to bat for the last over and held out.

LESLIE   That's right. We had a dresser who was a wonderful guy—gay as a brush—and we got him with a blackboard and chalk at the side of the stage, chalking up the score. The audience must have been absolutely baffled.

BRIAN   That was one of the best matches I've seen. At one time there was no chance of Jeff Jones ever having to bat and the night before he had a very good night out and he wasn't quite prepared for it. It didn't matter, because he didn't hit the ball with the bat. Every single ball hit him on the pad. There were six appeals for LBW. He thrust his leg out and it was the most marvellous last over. It won the series and we had great celebrations in the English Pub in Trinidad that night. Did you ever play for the Stage?

30

LESLIE   No. I am an old stager. I play for the Lord's Taverners. I've got a photograph of the late and great Kenny Barrington, saying, 'Thanks for helping with my benefit and for taking the greatest catch off my bowling I've ever seen.'

BRIAN   That's rather nice. Wasn't he lovely, though, Ken?

In your career, which do you prefer? Standing up in front of the curtains? Is that your favourite?

LESLIE   Anything is my favourite, I don't really mind—in a farce or a play or after-dinner speaking, a variety act, cabaret, pantomime—that's great, because you've got the lot there. Everyone thinks pantomime's easy and it's the most difficult convention.

BRIAN   Can I reveal, for the first time in public, that last week I was rung up and offered the part in pantomime of Alderman Fitzwarren this winter.

LESLIE   You're joking! Oh!

BRIAN   And I think it was going to be at a very nice theatre. I said I'd rather be Baron Hardup, but he said, 'No, you've got to be Alderman Fitzwarren,' and unfortunately this January I've already mapped something out. It's a thing I've been dying to do all my life.

LESLIE   You'll have to wear tights, you know, if you're Alderman Fitzwarren.

BRIAN   What Fits Warren fits me. But

31

pantomime is hard work, isn't it? You've got to do those twice-daily things.

LESLIE   Oh, yes. You clock in at two and clock out at half past ten at night.

BRIAN   Have you ever managed to bring cricket into your act?

LESLIE   I've got masses of cricket stories. The first time I met Fred, in fact, I was doing a cricket ballet. There was a ballet-dancing wrestler called Ricky Starr, so I did this burlesque. If you can have a ballet-dancing wrestler, why not a ballet-dancing cricketer? I did this thing from *Swan Lake* and ponced about in tights and a box and pads. Sheila Burnett was behind the wicket as the keeper. This was in the Fol-de-Rols.

BRIAN   Where are you from originally?

LESLIE   In fact I'm a Nottinghamshire man, born in West Bridgford, or bread-and-lard island, as it's called.

BRIAN   Not so far from Parr's Tree, then.

LESLIE   No, in fact Parr's Tree fell down when I was staying at the Bridgford Hotel, which is now council offices. I was in pantomime and there was this horrendous storm. Down went Parr's Tree and I went down in my pyjamas and dressing gown, got this hacksaw from the night porter and a torch and I climbed over into Trent Bridge. And I still have a branch of Parr's Tree.

BRIAN   They turned the rest of it into cricket bats, which they sold at enormous profit, but yours is the genuine branch.

LESLIE There is a poem in the Long Room—or square room, really—at Trent Bridge. It was written in 1938 to mark the centenary of cricket at Trent Bridge and it goes like this:

So small a space, so lost this slip of
    earth,
When we spread out the map that
    spans the shire
Only an oasis in a city's dearth,
A spark still left in long extinguished
    fire.
But men have gathered here and given
    their praise
To many a battle, many a Notts-shire
    team,
Stored up great sunlit deeds, then,
    going their ways
Have seen Trent Bridge for ever more
    in dream.
They helped to build a game, those
    cricketers,
The Gunns and Shrewsbury, Daft and
    Flowers,
Batting and bowling down the golden
    hours
On this hallowed turf. Surely today
Their ghosts come back where once
    they loved to play.
No cricket ground had nobler visitors.

BRIAN   That is super. Now, who wrote it?

LESLIE   Thomas Moult.

BRIAN   I must tell you, he wasn't reading that. Are you good at memorising lines?

LESLIE   Well, yes, because I started out as a straight actor—a lot of people think I still am!

BRIAN   You've managed to snatch an afternoon today, but how often can you get away to watch cricket?

LESLIE   My agent has arranged it very badly this year, because we started round about the time of the first Test and we finish working long after the sixth Test is over.

BRIAN   You had a match at Blackpool, though.

LESLIE   Oh yes. And what is amazing about coming up here to work is that if you're living down south you do tend to forget, unless you're reminded of it, and there's no reason why you should be, because it's not publicised in the papers, the fact that the Lancashire and Northern and Bradford Leagues—all these leagues—are unbelievably strong, play the most wonderful cricket and all have as a pro. a Test cricketer who just doesn't happen to be playing Test cricket for his country at the moment. There was this cricket festival at Blackpool. It was Geoff Boycott's World XI and an International XI and I just went along and, sure enough, there

34

were twenty-two players plus about eight reserves all of whom were Test cricketers from Sri Lanka, Pakistan, India, Australia—David Hookes was playing—it really was quite remarkable. I was asked to adjudicate the man of the match on the Sunday and there was no doubt about it that it was a guy called Sivaramakrishnan. He was turning the ball square.

BRIAN When the Indians come over next year, will you come and coach us in how to say that, because you've got it rather well. I'll call him 'Shivers'.

LESLIE It'll be 'shivers' anyway.

BRIAN You're wearing the MCC tie.

LESLIE The old ham and egg. It took me nine years of impatient waiting to get it and I've worn it ever since. I bought it seven weeks ago and I've worn it as a pyjama cord—I just love it.

BRIAN At one time it was not done to wear that tie until the great Lord Cobham became President of MCC in the mid-fifties and he said, 'What is the point of having a club tie if nobody wears it?' And he began to wear it and now everybody does. I think it's very good.

LESLIE I think it's a great honour to be a member of that particular club and to wear the tie. I'm not saying that sartorially it is the greatest choice of colours, but it's a smashing tie to wear.

BRIAN   A great honour to be in the club.
LESLIE   You're in the club, are you? You'll
make Fleet Street!

PROFESSOR SIR BERNARD LOVELL

In the mid-1980s I visited Jodrell Bank when doing a *Down Your Way* in Cheshire. I was amazed at the gigantic size of the revolving bowl of the telescope. It was not until I had finished my interview with Sir Bernard about Jodrell Bank that, over a cup of tea, I discovered his great interest in cricket. He had not only been a good cricketer but he had also carried out a number of highly technical experiments to try to help umpires in making their decisions. He emphasised that he was only trying to *help* them, not to usurp their powers. They are, and probably always will be, the final arbiters on all decisions.

None of his aids have so far been used in this country, partly due to the large expense involved. We now have a referee at all Tests and overseas there has been a third umpire watching the television replays, who can be called on if either umpire is in doubt about a run-out or a stumping. The difference between this and Sir Bernard's successful experiments, is that his method involves direct, and more or less instantaneous contact with the umpires. With the third umpire watching a monitor, decisions have taken up to 30 seconds as he watches several replays. Personally, so long as TV and the big screens on the grounds show replays, I think the umpires should be given Sir Bernard's aid to decide at least on run-outs and possibly stumpings. I hope you will find our conversation as fascinating as I did.

OLD TRAFFORD, 6 JUNE 1987

SIR BERNARD LOVELL I was given permission to take equipment to Jodrell Bank in 1945. It was very remote then and we were allowed to stay for a few weeks with these trailers. That was in December 1945 and we're still there. We started building the big steerable telescope in 1951/52. Before that I'd been building bigger and bigger aerials on the ground to try and do certain things and then the desire to make one of these devices completely steerable arose and that led to what you now see in the Cheshire Plain. We began operating in 1957 and this year we shall celebrate the thirtieth anniversary of its first use, which is really quite remarkable, because no one believed that it would be any good. In fact I had the greatest difficulty in persuading people either that it would last as an engineering structure for fifteen years, or that it would be useful scientifically, and now it's busier and more in demand than it ever has been.

BRIAN JOHNSTON Now, don't be modest about it, is it one of the great telescopes of the world?

SIR BERNARD I think it is. It's still one of the largest and I think remarkable as a scientific instrument because of its longevity. It cost us £600,000 to build and you may remember I got into a lot of trouble because of overspending. Now you couldn't possibly build it for less than £20 million. So it's one of the great investments of science.

BRIAN What's the greatest achievement you've seen in your time there? What gave you the most pleasure?

SIR BERNARD I think the answer must be, oddly enough, the detection of the carrier rocket of the first Sputnik in 1957 for the simple reason that it was the only instrument in the world that could do this by radar and it was the episode that got me out of trouble.

BRIAN Because it justified the expense.

SIR BERNARD Well, some solution to these problems then had to be found, because this was the first intercontinental ballistic missile. But, on the astronomical side, the fascinating thing is that if you go round the place today, you'll find the students and the staff working on maybe ten different projects and the things they're working on were entirely

39

unknown when we built the instrument in the 1950s. They've been the result of recent advances. So I think the great advantage of the instrument is that it has been so adaptable both to modern techniques and to the new discoveries which have subsequently been made and today it is a front-line instrument.

BRIAN   It is a very fascinating thing to see. It revolves completely round, does it?

SIR BERNARD That's right—about 3½ thousand tons, revolving with great precision on the railway track, just taking out the motion of the Earth. And of course the bowl, which is about 1½ thousand tons or thereabouts, is rotated on those columns which are as high as Nelson's Column.

BRIAN   What achievement that hasn't been achieved would you like to do?

SIR BERNARD   Well, I'd like to put the telescope into space. There's no problem in principle, but we're talking about billions of dollars. One of the next major developments in the subject with which I'm concerned is to put a large radio telescope, like the one at Jodrell, in orbit round the Earth and link it to the Jodrell telescope and to others round the Earth. This would give you the equivalent for some of these experiments of measuring the sizes of these remote objects in the universe of a telescope which had an aperture, instead of the 250 feet of our

Jodrell telescope, of 10,000 miles.

(Although the United States have subsequently put the Hubble telescope into space, it is an optical, rather than a radio telescope. There are hopes that a combined American/Russian project may put a radio telescope into orbit by the end of the century and there are Jodrell Bank scientists involved in that project. Ed.)

BRIAN   So that's played a big part in your life. Now let's come to cricket. You were educated down in Bristol, so did you play cricket as a boy down there?

SIR BERNARD   Oh, very much so. I spent—I was going to say 'wasted' ... But I nearly failed all my exams because of my enthusiasm for cricket.

BRIAN   We're not modest on this programme; how good were you as a boy?

SIR BERNARD   Well, I played for the university. I played as a bowler, but I made a few runs. I then got more interested in work, but I did play during the critical period of my first degree in Bristol. I played for three different teams, including the university. Nowadays, if one of my students told me he was doing that, I would have no time for him.

BRIAN   And did you see some Gloucestershire cricket in those days?

SIR BERNARD   Oh, very much so, yes.

BRIAN   Who particularly?

41

SIR BERNARD Hammond. I think I must have seen Walter Hammond play more or less his first match for Gloucestershire. One of my earliest memories is not of Gloucestershire but of seeing Hobbs make his hundredth hundred. That was in Bath, because the boundary between Gloucestershire and Somerset was close to my home. But I was a fanatical Gloucestershire supporter and indeed remained so until I became closely involved here at Old Trafford. Nevertheless, Somerset was also a great interest and then they had these tremendous hitters, Earle and Lyon.

BRIAN G. F. Earle—Guy Earle.

SIR BERNARD His bat looked like a toy. I thought of him yesterday, watching Botham. He was much bigger than Botham. But Hobbs—I think that is my earliest memory. I must have been a boy of about ten.

(*Sir Jack Hobbs made that hundredth hundred at Bath in 1923. At the time only W. G. Grace and Tom Hayward had ever reached that landmark. Ed.*)

BRIAN He was brought out a glass of champagne or ginger ale.

SIR BERNARD Something like that—by Percy Fender—and I believe given a cheque for 100 guineas. But Hammond was really the person that was so marvellous to those of us who were young.

BRIAN I was lucky enough to see him make

his 240 at Lord's against Australia in 1938 and I don't think the modern generation really appreciate how tremendous he was.

SIR BERNARD No, the cricket you see here is stodgy compared with that. His elegance was quite amazing. I remember one day Gloucestershire were playing Kent and I think either Freeman or Woolley got him out before he had scored and I was quite miserable. I almost went home for the rest of the day.

BRIAN When you came up here, then, what about Lancashire cricket?

SIR BERNARD Well, I came to Manchester and joined the university in 1936 and I discovered that the university was quite close to this ground and I used to get a bus down to the entrance. Where we are now, on top of this executive suite, is more or less on the site of the old galvanised shed. One used to pay sixpence to get in there. I saw quite a lot of cricket.

BRIAN Any particular Lancashire player you'd picked out?

SIR BERNARD Well, Cyril Washbrook, I remember. I've talked to him today and he's full of praise for some of the young people we might get in a few years' time. I remember him not only as a batsman, but also his fielding at cover point, which was quite spectacular.

BRIAN And you have some sort of office

43

here?

SIR BERNARD Well, I was very lucky to be made one of their vice-presidents about five or six years ago. So that's a very nice arrangement.

BRIAN Now, you've taken tremendous interest in the various technicalities of cricket and are trying to help the umpires. We can start with an easy one, because we can see it. There is your light meter, which looks like the top half of a clock. There are two of those on the Wilson Stand. How do they work?

SIR BERNARD We have a photosensitive element, which is transformed by some rather simple electronics into a small motor which drives that clock. The photosensitive element is more or less focused on the region of the sight screen and there you see what the light is. It doesn't pretend to be absolute, but it's relatively accurate.

BRIAN When it's up at twelve o'clock, is that perfect light?

SIR BERNARD No, the perfect light is when it's hard over at a quarter past. These are really crude experimental models. We've got a manufacturing design, but at the moment the TCCB are sitting on that, deciding what to do about it.

BRIAN People always say that you can't have a common thing like that, because the light on each cricket ground is different.

SIR BERNARD Well, of course they're different. But then you adjust this to suit the particular ground and from experience. You can't be absolute, because the umpire has to decide whether he offers the light to the batsman. It depends on the speed of the ball and all that sort of thing. It gives them a guide. You see, in the beginning, I thought it would be interesting to make a permanent recording of the light and about six years ago I had a light meter over the pavilion with a recording device and the intensity of the light came out on a paper chart. This was fascinating, because the conclusion one came to very quickly was that the umpires were rather consistent in the time at which they offered the light to the batsmen, but they were extremely inconsistent as to when they came back again. Very often the light would recover to what it was when they went off and another ten or fifteen minutes would elapse before they came back again. Now you have the recording here continuously. These are very sensitive. A cloud comes over and you will see them ... in fact, at the moment the light is better at the Warwick Road end than it is at this end. But I doubt if a batsman would notice that. These models won't last for ever, because they're very experimental; the sort of thing that scientists do with some bits and pieces. Every time I come here I look with some anxiety to see if

45

they're still working. They're all right at the moment. They are the result of a sort of evolution. In the beginning we had a radio link which became interfered with, I think, by BBC television transmissions and things like that. But now we've overcome that and they're very reliable.

BRIAN And I think it's terribly good for the public. They can at least see just what is being done to them.

(The light meters continued to function efficiently at least until the end of the 1992 season when the old Wilson Stand was demolished to make way for a new one. They are being rebuilt on the Red Rose and Executive stands, so that they are in line with the pitch. Ed.)

SIR BERNARD I started the light meters off, but then I was asked by the TCCB to investigate the possibility of electronic aids for umpires other than light meters.

BRIAN When I came to see you in your office at Jodrell Bank, you'd just had a meeting with two umpires and you asked them a simple question. How could you best help them?

SIR BERNARD David Constant and Don Oslear. They were very nice and they said that the things that worried them were, on the LBW law, whether the ball really would have hit the wicket if the batsman hadn't been in the way.

46

BRIAN Which they can't tell.

SIR BERNARD They said, 'Look, we can tell you whether the ball has pitched in the right place or whether it's going to go over the top of the wicket, if you can give us some indication if it would have hit the wicket.' Well, this was a fascinating problem—a very difficult one. The TCCB financed a feasibility study with a firm we knew in the south-east of London and this study was presented to the Board last summer and I heard recently that they decided to do nothing about it. It is rather expensive.

BRIAN What does it involve? Is it cameras?

SIR BERNARD You need very sensitive cameras of the type you use on your television and the computational problem is quite difficult.

BRIAN And at each end of the ground you'd have to have two?

SIR BERNARD You'd have to have four cameras to do this and the communication with the umpire would be quite simple. One would show lights on a board, for example.

BRIAN And would that be instant?

SIR BERNARD Absolutely instant.

BRIAN The ball hits the pad; there's a shout of 'How's that?' How long would it be before he could say?

SIR BERNARD This is one of the problems, that the computation would have to be done at very high speed. You can't keep the umpires waiting. But this problem is solved and each installation would cost somewhere between a hundred and two hundred thousand pounds. Incidentally, doing this, one becomes aware of the immense power and accuracy of the human eye. People say that computers can do everything. The umpires are jolly good. You have to do a very expensive design of equipment to give an answer equivalent to what the eye can do.

The other problem that interested the umpires was caught behind. I asked some of the Test Match cricketers and some of them were most unhappy that they had been given out erroneously on many occasions because they hadn't touched the ball. We have also solved that. This means inserting something in the bat and a few weeks ago here at Old Trafford I tested what I thought was going to be the final development model. I tried it in the nets and the first ball the whole thing more or less disintegrated. It's a very sensitive device.

BRIAN   Inside the handle of the bat would it be?

SIR BERNARD   That's right. And from there you transmit a signal to the umpire. He has an earphone.

BRIAN   That does sound good. Are you going to do it again?

SIR BERNARD   Oh yes. The TCCB are still interested and the problem is mine and that of the firm who are doing this. We have to produce this final model so that it will withstand the impact of the bat on the ball.

BRIAN What do the bat manufacturers say?

SIR BERNARD Well, we haven't asked them, but it's a very small device—something about as big as your little finger. The miniaturisation of modern electronics is quite astonishing.

BRIAN What about the other controversial one, which shows up on these big screens they have in Australia—the run-outs. They can be very difficult to judge with the human eye.

SIR BERNARD Well, that's very easy. The device which would do the LBW decision could easily do that as well. That would be an easier problem than the LBW decision. This would be an electronic decision from the video responses of the cameras as to where the bat and the crease are in relation to the ball hitting the stumps. But you're quite right, this is another thing that worried the umpires. A lot of things are easy if you're prepared to spend money.

(A straightforward experiment with a third umpire watching video playbacks of run-outs and stumpings was introduced for the South Africa v. India series of 1992/93. Light meters which show the worsening light on a series of illuminated lamps, rather than Sir Bernard's system, have been introduced on most first-class

grounds in England, although this system was tried at Old Trafford several years ago and discarded in favour of the more accurate clock-type meter which will continue to operate there. The LBW and caught-behind devices have been shelved because of expense. Ed.)

SIR BERNARD I think if these devices ever went into use, there would be many more decisions against the batsman, because the umpires always give him the benefit of the doubt.

BRIAN Which is right.

SIR BERNARD Which is right, but I think the batsmen would probably be rather annoyed, because they would be given out legitimately but they might not think so. But I do think it would save a lot of these irritating uncertainties. Of course the umpire's decision is always final. There never has been any suggestion of taking the decision away from the umpire. It's a matter of giving him some assistance in the things he really needs.

PETER SCUDAMORE

For some reason many jockeys seem to be mad about cricket, especially the jumpers, as opposed to the flat. Their season gives them a short break during the summer so that they are able to play or watch cricket and run a very useful jockeys' team, which plays for charity. At Headingley in 1989 I was able to say with *some* truth, 'We are very lucky to have a leg-spinner in the box with us today. He also happens to be quite a useful National Hunt jockey.' In fact Peter, in the season just finished, had ridden 221 winners, breaking the previous record by 72.

We commentators often think that we are busy, but what about this? Peter had flown in from New York that very Saturday morning having ridden at Belmont on Friday. He had only agreed to go to America, provided they guaranteed he would be able to get to Headingley by Saturday lunchtime. After watching the afternoon's play he was due to go down to Cheltenham to ride in two exhibition races against Willie Shoemaker the next day. Although he had a pale complexion, he looked pretty well on it all, and his sparse wiry figure put all of ours in the box to shame.

HEADINGLEY, 10 JUNE 1989

PETER SCUDAMORE I wouldn't have missed this for the world. My father's a great cricketing man and that's influenced me. We used to go and watch Worcester play when I was a child and a lot of cricketers are friendly with the National Hunt jockeys. I think it's because we're on holiday when they're playing and they're on holiday when we're out riding, so they come racing, we go cricketing and so you get to know some of the players.

BRIAN JOHNSTON So how much cricket have you managed to get this summer?

PETER I've played twice this summer. I've been lucky enough to play for the Starlight XI, raising money for terminally ill children. It's the brainchild of Eric Clapton.

BRIAN What sort of chaps do you have playing with you?

PETER Well, the last couple of times I've been out I've been bowled by Ian Bishop, the West Indies fast bowler—one of his leg-spinners, but it came very quickly to me at any rate (that's my story)—and Derek Underwood's first ball of the season absolutely clean bowled me.

BRIAN You didn't drive it through the covers.

PETER Well, I went to.

BRIAN Where do you bat normally?

PETER Anywhere I can, basically.

BRIAN And you like a bowl; do you give it a bit of a tweak?

PETER I do, yes. Colin Cowdrey called them tweakers. I think they're definite leg-spinners.

BRIAN And how much do you manage to watch. Do you support Worcestershire still?

PETER Yes, I follow Worcestershire very closely. But I get to know a lot of the county cricketers. I know Andy Stovold very well and some of the Gloucestershire boys, so I follow them and I know the Warwickshire boys—Andy Lloyd's a great racing man.

BRIAN Of course, you live in Gloucestershire.

PETER Yes, I've got the three counties all round me, very close.

BRIAN Do you have any particular heroes?

PETER The Scudamore family are great Botham fans. We follow Botham avidly. The editor of the *Sporting Life*, Monty Court, rings up and says, 'Botham should be dropped from the England team,' and we argue the other way for hours on end.

BRIAN Your father, Michael Scudamore, rode a Grand National winner.

PETER   He won the National and the Gold Cup. He was second in the championship one year to Fred Winter, so I had a bit to follow.

BRIAN   But, remarkably, I can't find that you've ridden the winner of the Grand National or the Gold Cup.

PETER   No, that's all to do yet.

(*And it was still all to do at the start of the 1992/3 season. Ed.*)

BRIAN   Did you ever think that 221 winners in the season was going to be possible? I think Jonjo O'Neill's 149 was the previous highest.

PETER   I was obviously lucky I was riding for two top stables—Charlie Brooks and Martin Pipe. Martin had two hundred winners himself, which is a record. The season set off very well. It's just like making your runs at cricket, you like to get your first winner, it's like getting your first run—and then hit a few sixes—get a few trebles and four timers—and you can say to yourself, 'If you keep up this average, you're going to ride two hundred winners.' But you don't actually believe it. Then it starts to materialise in mid-winter and people start saying, 'You'll ride two hundred winners.' You tend to get over the bigger races and then, come April time, concentrate on the two hundred.

BRIAN   You're making it sound very easy,

but that's ten months of hard work—or more. How much time do you have off between the end of one season and the start of another?

PETER We get most of June and most of July off—about ten weeks. But it's like being a cricketer or in the theatre, it's wonderful to get paid for doing something you enjoy.

BRIAN We rather feel that up here, but we don't like to tell our bosses that. You're taller than I expected. How tall are you?

PETER I'm about five foot eight, which is about the right size, as long as I don't eat too much.

BRIAN Well, what's your average weight?

PETER I ride at ten stone, which is the minimum weight that we have to ride at. So I have to get my bodyweight down to about nine stone nine pounds—that's with the saddle and all the equipment.

BRIAN Well, tell us the ghastly routine that you have to get to that. It absolutely terrifies me. Give us a daily diet.

PETER I wouldn't eat breakfast, because you're either travelling or riding out at that time of the day. If I've got a light weight, I wouldn't eat lunch, so I wouldn't eat till the evening. People say, 'Oh, you're silly not eating till the evening,' but it's my immediate weight loss that I'm worried about.

BRIAN How hungry are you getting by then? I should be absolutely ravenous.

55

PETER By the evening you're getting hungry, but it's the matter of doing things. I couldn't diet without doing something.

BRIAN Well, Scuders, it's tremendous discipline, undoubtedly. And when you do have your evening meal, is it a good tuck-in? Yorkshire pud and roast beef?

PETER No. You concentrate, obviously, on not too many chips or white bread. I tend to eat spinach. I find it a great help to me.

BRIAN Old Popeye found it a good idea.

PETER He did. I try to eat a lot of fish and lean meat.

BRIAN It doesn't sound very attractive to me, but now you've got time off, so are you getting a better diet?

PETER Well, you get used to it and whatever I put on I've got to get off, so I don't like to put too much weight on during the summer. It's not too bad. It's just one of the disciplines that we have and it's just there in the back of your mind all the time. I just don't over-indulge.

BRIAN Can you give us a typical day in the winter months when you're riding out and racing?

PETER One of the great things about it is that you don't have a typical day. It's like asking Goochie what his typical day is. What your typical day would like to be is getting up late and going to Cheltenham to ride three winners.

BRIAN   It doesn't happen. You get up early to ride out somewhere.

PETER   Two or three times a week I'm riding out at Charlie Brooks' or Martin Pipe's. I go and school and it usually means setting off fairly early in the morning—six o'clock-ish. Then I school up until probably breakfast time, usually arriving in the yard at about half past seven. Then I go and ride them over some jumps—usually teaching the young horses.

BRIAN   You're teaching them. That's part of the thing, is it?

PETER   Yes. The mutual benefit is so that I can trust the horse, I know what he's going to do and he can get used to me a little bit.

BRIAN   I asked you before we came on the air what happened in New York and whether you'd ridden the horse before and you said you hadn't. How important is it to know the horse before you ride it?

PETER   I got to New York yesterday and I found out all that I could about the horse. It is difficult. The horse I was riding yesterday was held up for a late run. Well, you don't know what your opposition are going to do, so you're guessing a little bit.

BRIAN   Do you let it snuffle you? Do you blow up its nose?

PETER   Doing a Barbara Woodhouse?

BRIAN   Have you ever tried that with a horse?

PETER   I always go up and give him a pat. I think if they trust you to start with you're better off. Give them a pat, try and make friends and say, 'Please—let's you and I get round safely here.'

BRIAN   Well, you don't always get round safely. You've had quite a lot of body damage. What sort of things have you got which haven't been hurt? You mustn't mention them all.

PETER   I've been hurt a few times. But coming back last night on the plane they showed the Centenary Test in Australia when Randall made 174 and they showed Lillee bowling and I think I would definitely rather do what I do than face Lillee or Holding or one of those bowlers.

BRIAN   That was a marvellous Test, where Randall rather baited Lillee, didn't he?

PETER   It was very funny. The bouncers were coming in and he was falling over backwards and pushing his hat onto the back of his head. You forget actually what a great batsman he was.

BRIAN   I emulated something. You remember in 1981/82 you were leading the championship and you fell off and broke your arm and John Francombe drew level with your number of winners a few weeks later and threw away his saddle and said, 'I'm not riding again.'

PETER   Yes, that's right.

BRIAN   I did that when I was doing *Down Your Way*. I gave it up at the same total as Franklin Engelman. I copied what John Francombe did, because old Jingle up there couldn't do anything about it and you weren't able to do anything in hospital.

PETER   It was a marvellous sporting gesture by John and that's what sport's about, isn't it?

BRIAN   Well, it is. In cricket on the field it's a bit rough sometimes and off the field it's friendly. What about jockeys? It's a very physical game, isn't it?

PETER   It's the same. Early on in a race people try to help each other, but you come to a certain point in the race where it's really business and you don't expect help.

BRIAN   But out in the country if you're going along in the lead with someone, do you have a chat with them?

PETER   Yes. It's not quite cantering along in the English country sunshine, but you'll help one another, give a little bit of room and manoeuvre not to upset one another. But at a certain point of a race then there's no mercy and if you get done or get hurt, well, that's what you accept before you go out.

BRIAN   What's the best horse you've ever ridden?

PETER   Probably Celtic Shot, because I won the Champion Hurdle on him and that's the best hurdling race and the best

59

championship race I've won, but I've been lucky to ride some very good horses.

BRIAN The difference between hurdling and the big fences—which do you prefer?

PETER I don't mind as long as I ride a winner over each. It's a great thrill to ride a good steeplechaser. I've ridden Burrough Hill Lad and Corbière—as good jumpers as I've ever sat on.

BRIAN How old were you when you first learnt to ride? Were you taught in an orthodox way? Did you have fairly long stirrups as a boy?

PETER Yes, I learnt the orthodox way. I never really had riding lessons. My father was always the sort of tutor in the background, but never actually gave me a lesson. I just picked it up. As long as I can remember I've ridden and played cricket. One's gone one way and one's gone downhill.

BRIAN You've just said you wouldn't have liked to have played Lillee, but would you have preferred the life of a professional cricketer?

PETER If I could dream about doing anything else, I would be a fast bowler.

BRIAN You've got slight aggression, haven't you? You've got to have to be successful.

PETER It's always appealed to me, the Lillee type, Holding type.

BRIAN What has happened to you in the

Grand National? How come you haven't won it?

PETER I always blame the horse. The trainer always blames me.

BRIAN Do you do the Fred Winter thing of staying on the inside?

PETER I've done it all ways. The closest I got was third on Corbière and then I looked like winning one year on a horse called Strands of Gold and I fell at Bechers. I was going on the inside then and everyone said that it was because I was going on the inside that I fell.

BRIAN So next year you went on the outside.

PETER And got beaten. It's one of the goals. I would love to do it.

BRIAN How different is it riding in the Grand National from riding in an ordinary steeplechase at Haydock Park or somewhere like that?

PETER You go slightly slower and horses tend to look at the fences a little bit more, because they're big and they're different and most times horses jump better for it. People say, 'Oh, the Grand National must be frightening,' but sometimes you can have a better ride round there than you can normally.

The man who valets me in the weighing-room—when we're in the weighing-room we have valets who clean all our tack and make sure we go out on time and in the right colours—is John Buckingham. He won the National on Foinavon. He's quite a good cricketer and tells some of the best cricketing stories that I know.

BRIAN Tell us one if you can remember.

PETER The Jockeys' XI were playing in Derbyshire against a local league side, which included Alan Ward, who had broken down and was having a bit of a comeback. And the local side batted first and made 250 or so and then the jockeys went in to bat and Alan Ward bowled early and knocked about three down very cheaply. So they gave the jockeys a bit of a chance. It began to look as if they were going to get the runs. They were about six wickets down and David Nicholson and John Buckingham were nine and ten, sitting there, waiting to go in. Then Alan Ward comes back on, bowling very fast and knocks the next one out. David Nicholson, who's always captain and a very, very keen cricketer, turns to John Buckingham and says, 'Come on, you're in.' John says, 'Hang on, I'm number ten. You're number nine.' 'I'm captain,' he says. 'You're number nine.' In he goes and Alan Ward starts walking back and, as he turns, John walks away. 'Hold on,' he says, 'I don't go that far on my holidays.' I think he lost his sense of humour with that, Alan Ward. He came roaring in and bowled one at John who jumped out of the way. It hit him on his bottom and bounced out for four runs. He was very pleased. And the other great story he tells is when he was umpiring and David Nicholson was bowling. John had broken his leg. David Nicholson comes roaring in and hits this player on the pad and appeals to John and John says, 'Not out.' John, because of his broken leg, is sitting on a shooting stick and David walked back past him, kicked the shooting stick from beneath him and said, 'Rubbish.'

JOHN KETTLEY

The weather plays a vital part in cricket. Ask Dickie Bird. He knows! So we thought that it was about time that we had someone who could forecast for us whether rain would stop play. We were lucky to find that the youngest of the weather forecasters was also a very keen cricketer, and needless to say it was raining when he joined us in the box at Old Trafford. I think they do a super job with their live, off the cuff, commentaries on local showers, high winds and depressions. I have never heard them make a gaffe as we (occasionally!) do at cricket. But in the days when they used magnetic devices to put letters or logos on the weather board one of them did slip up once. He was sticking letters all over the board showing where there would be RAIN, WIND, SHOWERS or FOG. As he tried to put FOG on to the board, the 'F' came unstuck and fell to the ground, leaving 'OG' over south-east England. He finished up with: 'So the outlook for tomorrow is still unsettled, with some strong winds—and I'm sorry about that "F" in FOG!'

OLD TRAFFORD, 29 JULY 1989

BRIAN JOHNSTON Well, if you presented this weather, you know what you can do with it. You are from Yorkshire.

JOHN KETTLEY Born in Halifax.

BRIAN Are you a committed Yorkshireman?

JOHN There's no choice—I am a Yorkshireman. I never lived in Halifax, I was just born in hospital there and lived in Todmorden. Many people will know that Todmorden is just about twenty miles from here. It's the border town. Administratively, of course, it's under Lancashire, in some respects, but not others. We're the only Yorkshire team in the Lancashire League. We've always been known as the border team, but there's no doubt about it, anybody who lives there is really a Yorkshireman.

BRIAN So did you learn your cricket there?

JOHN I'm still learning my cricket, Brian. It's very difficult to put it together sometimes, but yes. I did start as a very young boy. In fact I was taken round in my pram by my dad when I was a baby—all round the ground at Todmorden.

BRIAN What sort of cricketer are you? What's your forte?

JOHN I laughingly call myself an all-rounder, which means to say that if I fail with the bat, I've still got a second chance. So I do a bit of both—a bit of batting and a bit of bowling.

BRIAN You've brought these Lancashire League handbooks along with you. One's for '61 and one's for '56.

JOHN Well, the '56 one you'll see me appearing in—I was only four at the time, but I was taken round by my dad and saw all these really good cricketers. Everton Weekes was playing at Bacup at that time. But 'Lancashire Cricket League', priced ninepence in 1961, is the first one I really remember. I was doing a lot of scoring in those days.

BRIAN Some wonderful pictures of some young people who played in the league there—Hughie Tayfield, Everton Weekes, Harry Halliday.

JOHN I played in the league—mainly second and third team, it must be said. I only ever played in the first team once. It's the story of my life, really. I was selected for the first team in about 1969 or 1970. Peter Marner was the pro., who used to play here and went to Leicestershire.

BRIAN Hit the ball well.

JOHN Certainly did. But that game I was

selected for it rained all day long. The game was called off about four o'clock. My card playing improved.

BRIAN   It counted as being in the first team, anyhow.

JOHN   Oh, I think it did, but nobody remembers, of course.

BRIAN   But you still play cricket in charity matches. You're in much demand. Have you got a regular team?

JOHN   I play for a village called Ardeley, which is very near Stevenage.

BRIAN   My sister married the son of the people who used to live at Ardeleybury. It wasn't a great cricket ground. I played cricket there against the village.

JOHN   We've actually lost our ground, now. We were kicked off it last season. We now use a recreation ground at the next village called Walkern. It's actually a football ground in the winter. Variable bounce is the most accurate way of describing our pitch.

BRIAN   How often are you doing the weather?

JOHN   We have three shifts. One morning shift, broadcasting domestically and then we have the afternoon shifts, one into Europe and one into BBC1 and BBC2. The broadcast for Europe many people here wouldn't ever have seen, because we're broadcasting to Superchannel on the satellite and we're also broadcasting to the forces in

Germany.

BRIAN   How long does the preparation take?

JOHN   We've got a poky little office and we have a camera in there. We put the whole lot together and we do our own graphics. We sit at the console all day long, that's why we're all blind.

BRIAN   Do you make all the marks on the maps?

JOHN   Yes, we do everything. We couldn't possibly go in there cold one morning at seven o'clock and do a broadcast at ten past, because we have to get all this information together and put it into graphical form.

BRIAN   I watch your hand with fascination because you have a little clicker.

JOHN   That's right. We change the picture when we want to. That's the wonderful thing about it—we control our own destiny.

BRIAN   So how long did it take you to learn about the weather? Is there a weather school?

JOHN   We have a college at Shinfield Park near Reading. We are employed by the Met. Office, of course, and we go down there for refresher courses. I must be due for another one if it's raining on a Saturday at Old Trafford. We go down there for several weeks at a time on courses, just to see what the latest research is doing and whether we can actually still do it properly.

BRIAN   And the actual things you say—those are your own words?

68

JOHN Absolutely, yes. We don't have a script or anything like that. There's no autocue. We don't read anything. We just make it up as we go along. It's got to agree with the forecast coming out of headquarters—the engine room at Bracknell. They're providing us with the latest computer information, which says, for instance, if a band of rain coming across tomorrow is going to reach Manchester at five o'clock in the afternoon and we can't go on and say it's going to arrive in Manchester at three o'clock, otherwise we'd get our backsides kicked. But essentially we present the weather as we wish. We present it in the nicest possible way to explain the situation to the public.

BRIAN Are you allowed to crack any jokes? What's the best joke you've cracked?

JOHN I can't remember jokes, Brian. But I do like to be fairly light-hearted on television. I think if your own personality comes across, that's the main thing. I was told when I did my first audition in BBC Midlands back in 1980, 'Nobody's invited you into their lounge, so you've got to go in there and be pleasant. You mustn't upset anybody. Be yourself and don't try to copy anybody else.' It was a great temptation, when I first started down in London, to copy who I thought was the best—that was Jim Bacon at the time. But, what's the point.

You can't be another Jim Bacon. You've got to be your own personality.

BRIAN Is there a Big Brother listening and watching who rings up afterwards and says, 'Not bad, Ketters, but if I'd been you I'd have said a little bit more about those storms coming in from the east'?

JOHN Yes, we've got our people at Bracknell who monitor everything. I think they record every broadcast and it is quite strict, but on the whole they do trust you. They've got to trust you—they're the people who put you on in the first place.

BRIAN I'm sure you get ninety-nine per cent right, but has there been a one per cent where you've made a most terrible bloomer, said it was going to be the most glorious day tomorrow and it's pelted down all day? Don't be afraid of revealing—Big Brother's not listening.

JOHN It does occur and I think the public know that we're not trying to get it wrong.

BRIAN Where were you before the famous 1987 storm? Were you on that night?

JOHN I was on the breakfast time of the storm, travelling in to do it at four o'clock that morning. The A1 was like a chicane. There were trees all across the road and of course there were no traffic lights working in London that morning, so it was a really hairy journey. We were in Lime Grove in those days and everybody was standing outside with candles when I got there and a great cheer went up, 'Here he is. The man who's responsible for all this.' There'd been a power cut inside the studio, so we went up to Television Centre to do the broadcast from a little annexe. I was due to start on the air at five to seven and my shift finished at nine. I was doing updates with no graphics at all about every twenty minutes about how the storm was going. And I was still there at two o'clock in the afternoon, doing little updates.

BRIAN People do tend to blame you, don't they?

JOHN Yes, they do, but it's like expecting the bus to be on time. Everybody knows the bus is always late. It's just an old-fashioned thing that's carried on for ever.

BRIAN We talk of long-distance forecasting. Had I come to you in May, would you have forecast this glorious summer?

JOHN Oh, I did. I'm sure I told you that. I had a hunch, actually, because it was an odd year—'89—that it was going to be a good one. And we'd had two very mild winters. It was only a hunch and I would not have dared go on television and say so.

BRIAN And I believe you said, if you remember, 'Except on Saturday 29 July, when it may drizzle during lunchtime at Old Trafford.'

JOHN Well, we should have played this Test a week ago.

71

BRIAN   Now, you are one of the few people who've been mentioned in a hit at the top of the pop charts.

JOHN   It was a rather boring title called 'John Kettley is a Weatherman', which is open to debate. But it could have been the end of a wonderful career and the start of a new one. But I never really got into the music industry. It was a band called the Tribe of Toffs who wrote to me in about February last year and said they'd got this song together. I questioned whether it was a song at all.

BRIAN   Can you remember the words?

JOHN   There weren't many. 'John Kettley is a weatherman. John Kettley is a weatherman. And so is Michael Fish.' Since that day Michael Fish thinks the song is about him.

BRIAN   Now let's go back to Yorkshire. Who have been your real favourites there?

JOHN   He's not here at the moment, but when I was a kid Freddie Trueman was my hero. And then I must admit, even though things were a little unsettled at Yorkshire in recent years, Geoffrey Boycott became a hero as well.

BRIAN   Well, he was a marvellous player. You could admire the technique.

JOHN   Since then it's been difficult to have heroes, because they're not really performing as we'd like them to perform. But they're a

72

great bunch of lads and nothing would give me greater pleasure than to see Yorkshire a fine side again.

BRIAN Do you go and watch them?

JOHN When they pop down south. I went to Lord's last year for the county match on a Wednesday afternoon. It was a nice day, but there weren't many people on the ground. I was walking towards the pavilion and David Bairstow saw me, so I had to go and join them in the dressing room. That particular day Yorkshire were having a bad time of it and Kevin Sharp was the twelfth man, but he had done something to his back. He really was in a bad state and he was on antibiotics. So that day I almost went out subbing.

BRIAN Would that have been the climax?

JOHN That would have been absolutely wonderful.

BRIAN Walking along the street, do people stop you and say, 'What's it going to be like for our fête next Saturday week?'

JOHN Yes. It's nice in a summer like this. People ask about wedding days and they think you know months and months ahead. I think about it first and then I'll say, 'Yes, it looks as if it's going to be OK. I think the temperature—not as high as it is now, of course—about twenty-one degrees—seventy. A bit of cloud, but yes, it should be fine.' Because that stops them worrying about the weather.

73

BRIAN When you work out the centigrade and Fahrenheit thing, it doesn't quite work out the way I do it, which is to double it and add thirty.

JOHN No, but it's not far away. We do tend to remember all the conversions now, with years of practice.

BRIAN At thirty-three centigrade what is it?

JOHN Ninety-two.

BRIAN Under my method it would be ninety-six.

JOHN The bigger the number, the more out it will get. But sixteen-sixty-one is a good one to remember. You just reverse the numbers: 16—61.

BRIAN What happened then?

JOHN Oh dear. This is the end of a promising interview.

BRIAN 1661?

JOHN Not in 1661, Brian. Sixteen Celsius is sixty-one Fahrenheit.

BRIAN I was thinking something might have happened to Charles II then.

JOHN There's another one: 28—82.

BRIAN Oh, I'll be able to do that. What are the finer parts of the British Isles as regards weather?

JOHN Apart from St John's Wood, of course, the south coast of England is probably just about the driest. But the east of Scotland usually does extremely well— surprisingly well. They do get this horrible 'haar' effect off the North Sea. This low cloud and cold wind sometimes, but they actually get very good shelter from the Grampians.

BRIAN Are we too unfair? There's always the joke about rain at Old Trafford.

JOHN Well, they get about thirty-five inches of rain here a year, I think, off the top of my head. It is cloudier up here in the north-west of England, but the rain isn't necessarily all that heavy. The Lake District probably bears the brunt of most of the rain. That's why it's so green. But I thought you were going to ask me about this England team.

BRIAN Well, do you have a quick solution?

JOHN It would be nice if there was more pride put back into English cricket by having people wearing caps, like the Australians do.

MAX JAFFA

I was especially pleased when Max Jaffa accepted to be our guest at the Oval in 1989. I had known him as a brilliant violinist who entertained holidaymakers at Scarborough for twenty-seven years, and had listened to him and his trio for even longer on their regular BBC broadcasts. What I did not know was his love of cricket. He and his wife, Jean, had lived in Elm Tree Road, St John's Wood, for thirty-two years before he so sadly died in 1991. From his house in the shadow of the Grandstand it was perfectly possible to lob a cricket ball over the wall into Lord's. But strangely I seldom if ever saw him there. For some reason he preferred the Oval and was a strong supporter of Surrey. He also was a regular at the Scarborough Festival and other first-class matches on the famous ground at North Marine Road. He enjoyed meeting all the cricketers—usually in the Mayor's Tent—and was especially fond of Herbert Sutcliffe and Len Hutton. He even played in a charity match with Freddie Trueman but had to retire hurt with an injured Achilles' tendon—not Fred's fault!

I have given these cricket details because on reading our conversation, I find that I was so intrigued with his life story, that I almost ignored the cricket side of it.

One thing which perhaps did not come out in our broadcast was what a great communicator he was. One of the joys of being at one of his concerts or listening to his broadcasts, was to hear his friendly, amusing and completely relaxed introductions to the various items. He was also a very modest man. Our billing in the *Radio Times* had described him as 'the popular musician'. He said he was delighted just to be called a musician, and he didn't demur when I suggested he should have been called 'the great fiddler'.

What made his visit to us at the Oval so special was that he was accompanied by his dear wife, Jean, who is not only a wonderful singer, but also a fabulous cook. To prove this she brought us a splendid chocolate cake, topped with strawberries and cream.

THE OVAL, 26 AUGUST 1989

BRIAN JOHNSTON Did you ever play cricket?

MAX JAFFA Oh, yes. My most memorable match was for the Guildhall School of Music XI, where I was a student, against the Royal

Academy. We won by seven runs. I was the last man in, to cat-calls of 'Watch those fingers'. I scored seven not out and we eventually won by seven. I remember it so well, because it's only a hundred years ago.

BRIAN What about this finger business? There you were, a budding violinist, playing cricket.

MAX I didn't play a lot of cricket. I watched a fair amount.

BRIAN Let's go right back to the beginning. Why did you start playing the violin? Were you bullied into it?

MAX I wasn't bullied into it. I had an extraordinary father. He was, I am sure, the original patriarch and on my sixth birthday he came into my bedroom to wish me happy birthday, handed me a fiddle and said, 'You're going to be a violinist'. And nobody ever argued with my father—certainly not at the age of six.

BRIAN So what did you do then?

MAX I sort of looked at it and looked at him and said, 'Well, thanks very much,' and thought if only he'd brought me a bat or a ball or anything.

BRIAN Was he musical?

MAX No, not a bit. There is no music in my family except my offspring and they're not professional. They are just very musical. My father hadn't a note of music in his entire body. But he was keen. He loved to listen and he did do me a very, very great favour. At the time I didn't realise it, but he took me to a concert at the Queen's Hall. We lived round the corner from the Queen's Hall. I was born in Langham Street, just by the BBC. By the way, while I think about it, this is a great day. On 26 August 1929, I did my first broadcast.

BRIAN At what age?

MAX Young.

BRIAN But how long did it actually take you to learn? When could you actually play the violin?

MAX I gave my first concert at the Pier Pavilion in Brighton aged nine. I've got a picture at which the entire family laugh every time they see it—and they ask to see it very often—of myself in a sort of velvet suit, clutching a fiddle.

BRIAN The little genius.

MAX Well, hardly.

BRIAN That's very young and you began conducting orchestras and leading orchestras in your teens.

MAX Yes, in fact in 1929 it was my orchestra from the Piccadilly Hotel and it was from there that I did my first series of broadcasts, which seemed to go on for ever. They broadcast from there once a week at lunchtime from one until two as, indeed, we are doing now.

BRIAN What was it that made you become

79

a leader?

MAX I wouldn't know. I've never thought about it. One doesn't lead. One's called a leader, but I think really and truly that's a misnomer.

BRIAN Well, they've got to have confidence and they've got to like you.

MAX I think you've got to be able to answer silly questions from other musicians like, 'Why do we have to do it up-bow? Why can't we do it down-bow?' And if you're a decent leader you say, 'Do it your way.'

BRIAN So from the Piccadilly in the early thirties, where did you go then?

MAX From there I graduated into the dance band world and I became the only violinist to lead a dance band for a then very, very popular dance band leader, Jack Harris.

BRIAN Did you enjoy that?

MAX Well, it was fun. Of course, I didn't play jazz. I think I was the straight man. I played the odd chorus in the way that the singer might sing it. But we're getting on towards the war, you see, and I felt I really couldn't win the war playing the fiddle. There had to be something I could do to win the war. I wanted to get into the RAF as aircrew, but, unfortunately, I was too old. So I joined the Artillery and I was a bombadier. I was stationed for a while on the heath at Blackheath. There were nine of us there. Seven gunners, one bombadier and a second lieutenant. We had a search light and a Lewis machinegun. The searchlight was to guide the German planes into London and the Lewis machinegun was to shoot them down if they were silly enough to come low enough. I got a bit fed up with that after a while, though. Then I began to answer every Army Council Instruction that came round asking for volunteers for this, that and the other. I volunteered for everything, including the Palestine police—that's one I remember with affection, because I was turned down for that one also. Eventually an Instruction came round asking for volunteers to transfer from the Army into the RAF for aircrew duties. Of course I volunteered and fortunately for me the qualifications asked for were not very high, so I was able to get in. I transferred to the RAF and eventually, after training at various stations, I got my wings in Rhodesia.

BRIAN Did you actually fly a plane?

MAX I flew 32 different types of plane. I'm very proud of that, actually. I got my wings in Rhodesia and did my operational training and went up to the desert and was finally sent home. There they said, 'You're too old to fly operationally.' They gave me the option of either becoming an instructor on Tiger Moths—and flying Tiger Moths was lovely, but the instructing on them I didn't really fancy, because if I'd got hold of any pupils that were as bad as I was, my life would be in danger. The other option was to join the Air Transport Auxiliary, who were ferrying pilots. They ferried aircraft from squadrons to maintenance units and back again. And I said I thought that would be rather nice and, as it turned out, it was better than rather nice. So I was discharged from the RAF and joined the ATA—not to be confused with the ATS.

BRIAN Amy Johnson was on the same job. Now, you haven't played the fiddle all this time. What happened to your fiddle?

MAX I sold it just before the war and the first thing I did with part of my gratuity when I came back was to buy a fiddle. But I hadn't really thought about the fiddle very much except for one very stupid occasion in Rhodesia when I was a bit the worse for drink and somebody said, 'I understand you play the fiddle.' I said, 'I used to.' He said, 'We have a symphony orchestra in Bulawayo. Would you play a concerto with us?' I said, 'Yes, of course,' and thought no more about it until the following morning, when I received a note thanking me for my offer to play the violin at their concert, which was in ten days' time. Not only had I not got a fiddle, I hadn't got my music and I hadn't played for a few years. However, I did it and I still have the programme. 'Acting Sergeant Max Jaffa, by kind permission of Group

Captain French, is going to be the soloist at tonight's concert.'

BRIAN How were the old fingers?

MAX Bunch of bananas. Absolutely ghastly. But I did sort of settle down. They found me a fiddle and they were very good about it. At the performance at Bulawayo Town Hall it was great, because the place was full and they were all on my side. I can't remember much about the concert, but, looking back on it, I should think the performance by the solo violinist was pretty dire. The orchestra were jolly good and well behaved.

BRIAN You say you bought a violin after the war. Is it the same one you've used ever since?

MAX No. I've still got it, but in 1947 I raised my sights a bit and thought it was about time I had a decent fiddle. I'd saved £600, but the one that I really liked was £1,200, so I went to my bank manager and he was very kind. That's the one I've used ever since with the odd day when I practise on the old one which is pretty bad, but it's good for practising.

BRIAN What is this—a Stradivarius?

MAX It's a Guarnerius, made in 1704. Somebody asked me if I got it when it was new. In fact most of the great violinists of today who have one of each prefer the Guarneri.

BRIAN I should be terrified of carrying it

83

around and dropping it.

MAX   I don't really think too much about it. Jean won't let me leave it in the boot of the car, locked up, if we go into a restaurant. She says, 'I'll carry the fiddle in.' I say, 'Leave the damn thing there, it's quite safe.' But I suppose she's right, of course.

BRIAN   Now we've got to deal with two things. The Grand Hotel—I don't know how many years you did that for the BBC—and then Scarborough.

MAX   The Grand Hotel, actually, I didn't do for very long, in fact for the shortest time of any leader of the Grand Hotel broadcast.

BRIAN   Well, why do we associate you with the Grand Hotel?

MAX   I don't know—maybe oranges and palms. But it's stuck.

BRIAN   And you played in Scarborough for how long?

MAX   Twenty-seven years. I was asked to do it. The Scarborough people got on to me 28 years ago and asked me to do this thing and I said, 'No, thank you very much.' I was rather busy and it was Jean who talked me into it, because she'd been up there as a guest artist. You know she's a jolly good singer. She said, 'You do it for one year and I promise to show you some of the loveliest countryside you've ever seen.' And I said I'd do it for one year and stayed 27. But coming back here to the Oval is boyhood memories, because

84

although I'm a Middlesex man born and bred and still live there, Surrey was always my team and I saw on this beautiful pitch—and it is a beautiful pitch—some of the greatest players of all time. The most wonderful cover point, who could also bat a bit.

BRIAN Hobbs.

MAX Yes. And Sandham and Strudwick.

BRIAN So you came more to the Oval than to Lord's.

MAX Oh, much more, yes. It's been a great joy looking out from this window in your palatial commentary box.

ERIC IDLE

We have had a number of comedians as our guests in 'A View from the Boundary'—Michael Bentine, Brian Rix, Willie Rushton, John Cleese, Leslie Crowther and Max Boyce. They all seem to love cricket and it's often the one thing in life which they take seriously. I am not so sure, however, that our guest at Trent Bridge, Eric Idle, did so. In fact, after meeting him I could not discover what he *did* take seriously, except perhaps for comedy itself, which strangely is a very serious business.

Mind you I am probably wrong in classifying Eric as a comedian. He is so many other things as well—writer, guitarist, composer and film star. At the time he was living in a large house in St John's Wood, not far from me, but only a penalty kick or so from Gary Lineker, one of the Wood's other most distinguished inhabitants.

On reading through the transcript of our conversation I suppose I should also award him the accolade of 'singer'. I also found fascinating his description of how Monty Python was put together. I told you comedy was a serious business.

I began by asking him about the tie which he was wearing.

TRENT BRIDGE, 9 JUNE 1990

ERIC IDLE This is actually a Pembroke College tie—which I borrowed from a garage attendant on the way up.

BRIAN JOHNSTON You were at Cambridge.

ERIC Yes, I put this on to remind you, so you would mention it and people would think I wasn't quite so eccentric.

BRIAN Did you perform at cricket at Cambridge?

ERIC No, I wasn't half good enough for that. I just performed on the stage. I wasn't even good enough to play for Pembroke.

BRIAN But you achieved a certain prowess there, because you were President of the Footlights. There must have been some famous names.

ERIC When I got there Tim Brooke-Taylor was President and I had to audition for him and Bill Oddie. John Cleese was there and Graham Chapman. The Frost had just left. *(David Frost. Ed.)*

BRIAN What do you do when you go to an audition?

ERIC We did a very bad sketch. I went with some other people who laughed all the way through and giggled and I didn't laugh. They thought, therefore, that I must have been funny.

BRIAN What has been your cricket connection? What county do you follow?

ERIC Warwickshire. I lived quite a lot of my early life there. The first game I ever saw was about 1953, Warwickshire against Australia. Freddie Gardner and Norman Horner opened the batting, I think, and I used to have one of those books and used to do all the dots and all that on the Rea Bank.

BRIAN Oh well, Frindall's getting a bit past it. Would you like to come and do it for us? So you went and watched. What about actual playing?

ERIC I was at school at Wolverhampton and we had a cricket pitch and I became a wicket keeper, because I realised fairly early on that you had gloves on. This was obviously much better. Also I tended to go to sleep on the boundary and if you're wicket keeper you know pretty certainly that it's coming in your direction every ball.

BRIAN It's essential to keep awake.

ERIC And much easier, because something's always about to happen. I broke my nose keeping wicket, which is why I have this rather handsome and eccentric profile.

BRIAN I thought it was a very distinguished nose. I was getting rather jealous about it.

ERIC It depends which side you look at.

BRIAN Keeping wicket can be quite dangerous. I was standing up to a moderately fast bowler and the batsman snicked it onto my nose. It's painful, isn't it?

ERIC It's very painful.

BRIAN What it does reveal is that both you and I stood up at the wicket. They don't nowadays, which is very cowardly. I know you're always travelling all over the world. Do you follow the cricket at all?

ERIC I love watching cricket, yes. Wherever England are losing abroad, I'm usually there.

BRIAN What about the film career? We've all seen you in *Nuns on the Run*. Was that fun to make?

ERIC It was an hysterical film to make. We spent most of the six or seven weeks dressed as nuns, walking round west London.

BRIAN What did you have on underneath?

ERIC We had our trousers and jackets. It was freezing. So you can whip it off and leave for home at once or nip into the pub quickly.

BRIAN Are they quite comfortable with that thing across your forehead?

ERIC They're horrendously uncomfortable. They're tight and only your face protrudes. You can't hear anything and you can't see anybody. If they approach you from behind it makes you jump. You can understand now why nuns take a vow of silence.

BRIAN What about old Robbie Coltrane, is he funny?

89

ERIC   Coltrane is hysterical. And he is huge. He's a very big man.

BRIAN   What do you like to be called? Writing is your basic business.

ERIC   Well, it was my basic business, but for the last five or six years I seem to have been doing nothing but acting. I like to be called a comedian, really.

BRIAN   In Monty Python you started writing, did you? And then you wrote yourself some good stuff I suppose.

ERIC   The whole thing about the Footlights is that you write and act. Nobody else is going to write for you, so you're virtually forced into writing for yourself. And we were very lucky. When we came down from Cambridge we got co-opted by Frost who dragged us off to write for him. We were writing his ad-libs for about ten years.

BRIAN   Do you mean to say you've written some of Frost's jokes?

ERIC   Some of Frost's best jokes. He still uses some of mine.

BRIAN   You're the chap I've been wanting to meet for years.

ERIC   I can let you have a few after dinner jokes, partially used.

BRIAN   What were all these people like, Michael Palin, Terry Jones and the late Graham Chapman?

ERIC   Chapman was a mad, pipe-smoking eccentric.

90

BRIAN John Cleese said you used to sit round the table and discuss the next Monty Python and all go away and write something completely different from what you'd agreed to write. Was that roughly it?

ERIC Usually, yes. You can't really map out comedy. It just has to come and you have to say, 'Well that works and that doesn't work.'

BRIAN How disciplined was it? Because it looked zany and inconsequential.

ERIC It was completely disciplined. We worked from about ten till five solidly and we never ad-libbed a word. It was always completely scripted. We did all the ad-libbing in the writing sessions, so we always knew exactly what we were going to say. The Footlights motto is 'Ars est colare artem'.

BRIAN Oh, quite. You needn't translate for me, but for the sake of the listener, would you mind?

ERIC I will translate. It's 'The art is to conceal the art', which is true, I suppose, of most activities in life.

BRIAN Why do I always think of the sheep in Monty Python?

ERIC Well, we always used to drop sheep on people's heads when things were going a bit slow.

BRIAN Why did you select sheep? Because they're harmless characters?

ERIC Well, they're very boring—sheep.

They stand around all day not doing much and then being eaten. It's hard to sympathise with them, isn't it? So being dropped on people's heads on television is relatively a stage up for a sheep.

BRIAN How long ago was Monty Python? It seems so recent.

ERIC It started over 20 years ago.

BRIAN And how many series did you do?

ERIC We did about 45 shows in all and we finished in about 1973, so we're already history.

BRIAN And then you made films.

ERIC We made films until about seven years ago and since then nothing really.

BRIAN And how different was it doing the telly and then films?

ERIC In television everything can go in, because you're going up to the last minute. Filming is so slow and you've got to get the script right. We'd always take two or three years to write the script and re-write it and re-write it. So it's all much more prepared and there's much less room for spontaneity to add things at the last minute.

BRIAN You took the micky out of the establishment always.

ERIC That was our job at the time and now we've become the establishment.

BRIAN Have people taken the micky out of you?

ERIC Oh, absolutely yes.

BRIAN   How many people copied Monty Python? It's been copied in various degrees, hasn't it?

ERIC   It's like a cricket team. We were the team at that time and now there's the current team. They remember you when they were kids and they say, 'Oh, that's why we became comedians.' In the same way, I imagine, as cricketers today say, 'We became cricketers because we saw Mr Trueman bowl.'

BRIAN   I always hope that the film you did called *The Life of Brian* was named after me.

ERIC   As a tribute, of course. I think you actually appeared in one of the sketches a long time ago.

BRIAN   Oh, I did—Peter West and myself. You took the micky out of us. Are you a team man, or are you happier performing individually?

ERIC   I am much happier in a team. I think essentially as a comedian I'm a wicket keeper.

BRIAN   But you have floated off into different films and things.

ERIC   Even in a film it's a team activity, really. I would never want to be a stand-up comic or just on my own.

BRIAN   Have you ever done that in cabaret or anywhere?

ERIC   The cabaret was at Cambridge. We used to do that at weekends and make quite a good living out of it.

BRIAN   Are you a good stand-up comic?

ERIC   No, hopeless. I'm terrible. I can write other people's jokes and one-liners, but it doesn't appeal to me. I like to hide behind a character and put on some make-up, or in Peter West's case I had a whole bald head to put on.

BRIAN   You tended often to be in drag.

ERIC   (*with a sigh*) I had the best legs, it has to be said. But with Python we'd just divide up the parts and whatever was going we'd grab. So usually by the time Cleese had taken all the bullying parts and the slapping cars and the hitting people about the head parts and Jones had taken the smaller parts, there were only a few women left, so I used to end up with those.

BRIAN   Going back to Warwickshire, Freddie Gardner, who you mentioned, was a great character, although he didn't appear to be one on the field. Did you mingle at all with the players?

ERIC   I think I saw them in Stratford once, but the only player I met in the early days was Tom Graveney, who was my great hero.

BRIAN   He's the ideal chap to have watched.

ERIC   Wonderful batsman.

BRIAN   You don't see so many like him.

ERIC   Well, I think Gower's in the same mould.

BRIAN   He's outstanding.

Now, I believe you play the guitar. The

fingernails of course are beautifully manicured. Do you use a pleckers—a plectrum?

ERIC I have a plectrum, yes.

BRIAN Is that cheating, or is it allowed?

ERIC It's totally allowed. Anything is allowed, I think—unless you get caught at it.

BRIAN Do you play for fun or just for yourself? Have you done it professionally?

ERIC I've done it semi-professionally. I came out of a fridge in *The Meaning of Life* and sang a song about the galaxy. I sang a catchy little ditty on the Cross—'Always Look on the Bright Side of Life', which I wrote.

(In The Life of Brian. *Ed.)*

BRIAN What about your voice. You've just performed Co-co in *The Mikado*. Did you enjoy doing that?

ERIC I loved doing Co-co. I did it at the English National Opera and then last November I went to do it in Houston, Texas.

BRIAN The Doctor produced you—Jonathan Miller. Was it very different from the orthodox?

ERIC I said to him, 'What are you going to do with *The Mikado*?' And he said, 'Well, I'm going to get rid of all that Japanese nonsense for a start.' Which is very good, since it's set in Japan. He made it entirely black and white, with dinner jackets and

95

thirties style. A cross between Fred Astaire and the Marx Brothers.

BRIAN Did you do one or two of the traditional twiddling dances which they used to do in Gilbert and Sullivan?

ERIC Well, I had to do quite a lot of dancing. I had seven songs and about four or five dances. You get 'Tit Willow', you get 'A Little List'—I used to re-write the list every day for the performance. I used to put whoever was in the news on the list that night and the chorus used to face me upstage and look at me, so that I'd always try and make them laugh.

BRIAN You were unlucky in a sense in that you missed the great music-hall period.

ERIC There was a bit of that around when I first started. I went to see Norman Evans in Manchester and Morecambe and Wise were just young comics then. Rob Wilton—that wonderful man with 'The Day War Broke Out'—I saw a bit of that. There were still music-hall acts.

BRIAN Have you ever modelled any of your female parts on Norman Evans?

ERIC He was very Python—he was huge.

BRIAN And he did that marvellous act like Les Dawson does today, with no teeth.

ERIC Well, I think Lancashire comedians are probably the best and certainly were the funniest.

BRIAN Oh, yes. If you just go through them

96

from Tommy Handley to Arthur Askey to Ted Ray—they're helped a little by the accent. If you tell a story in a Lancashire accent it sounds a bit funnier than if I tell it. You never saw Max Miller, did you?

ERIC No, but I adored his records. I used to play them regularly. I never saw him live and he wasn't allowed on television, was he?

BRIAN He was the great insinuator. He never quite got to the point and left it to people's imaginations. Nowadays people go a bit further.

ERIC He used to let the audience complete the joke, which is very clever: 'You're the sort of people who will get me into trouble! Now then, is this Cockfosters? No, madam, it's Max Miller's.'

BRIAN Oh, that one he didn't leave to the imagination.

What about alternative comedy, as they call it? Do you think sometimes they go a little too far? Or do you think you can't go too far?

ERIC I think it's the job of comedy to go just that bit too far. It's just to stir people up and make them laugh a bit and I think you have to go a little bit too far to do it. Then the line keeps moving as life continues. Python looks quite staid now—conservative.

BRIAN But the essential bit of your comedy was to shock, I think.

ERIC Well, yes, partially. It's too easy to do

that. We tried not to rely on just pure shock. There's a limited return on it. You can't just shock and keep shocking. So we'd always try to provide good laughs.

BRIAN What about *Baron Münchhausen*? That's a good film.

ERIC It's a lovely film. It was one of the most nightmarish experiences of my life. I had to have my head shaved. I was bald for six months. I was in Rome, being hung up in tanks, being blown up and suspended from the ceiling and it was total hell.

BRIAN Can you stay bald for a week, or do little tufts of hair start growing?

ERIC They have to shave it every day, otherwise it becomes like velcro and you can run into the wall and stick to it with your head.

BRIAN And how long did it take to recover from it to the fine head of hair that you've got now?

ERIC I am terribly butch, so it grew back quite quickly.

BRIAN Will you do anything for art, then?

ERIC Anything for a laugh is what I was accused of. Art? Yes, I think you have to. If you're doing something you have to plunge yourself totally into it to get it right.

BRIAN You live in St John's Wood, will you be going round the corner to Lord's this summer?

ERIC Yes. I hope to see Mr Gower

occasionally.

BRIAN He is great fun to watch. You probably like him because he's artistic—the touch player.

ERIC That's what the game's about for me. It's what makes the difference between that and baseball and anything like that. It's the class shot. You can't describe it, it's a thing of beauty—the good cover drive.

BRIAN I was delighted to hear that you've written a play about cricket. It's one of my ambitions. You have produced a musical comedy—not for the stage.

ERIC We wrote it originally for the stage and then we thought it would do very nicely on radio. It's called *Behind the Crease* and it's about the three things the English like most—sex, royalty and cricket—not necessarily in that order. I've written it with a friend of mine called John Du Pre and we did it with Gary Wilmott playing a West Indian hotel owner and I play a seedy journalist.

BRIAN A cricket writer? Or one who sits by the pool and takes notes of what goes on that shouldn't.

ERIC Exactly. It's all about entrapment. Which, of course, never happens.

BRIAN No, no. It wasn't, of course, based on any tour in the West Indies.

ERIC No, it just came to me while I was on holiday in the West Indies one year.

BRIAN   Is it easy to compose a cricket song?
ERIC   We did a lovely song which went:

Oh jolly good shot
Oh well played, sir
Oh well let alone
Oh he's hit him on the bone
Did it hit him on the head?
No it hit him on the leg
I think the fellow's dead
No he's getting up again
Oh it's just a bit of rum
No it's hit him on the bum
Is he out? Is he out?...

We should have had fifteen people singing this—very tightly.
BRIAN   That was very good—quick moving. Is there a wicket keeper's song? Why he missed a stumping, perhaps—a wicket keeper's lament?
ERIC   There should be a wicket keeper's lament.

Gary Wilmott is playing this hotel keeper at the Nelson Arms—'We turn a blind eye to most things.' It's set in 'the Wayward Isles', which I rather like. I play the seedy reporter who's trying to get something on this English cricketer called Brian Steam, who's a fast bowler. There's a seedy journalist's song, 'Strolling Down the Street of Shame':

I saw judge outside a judge's quarter
Messing with another judge's daughter.
I said, 'Hello, hello, me lud,
I'd keep this secret if I could,
But I have a moral duty as a reporter.'

BRIAN   Very good. It seems to be all sex so far.
ERIC   It's mainly sex. There are one or two bits of cricket in there.
(And finally Eric was persuaded to finish with a reprise of, 'Oh jolly good shot'. Ed.)

GEORGE SHEARING

One of the bonuses of my 47 years of cricket commentary has been the way it has brought me in close touch with the blind. From our letters we know that we have thousands of blind listeners, who rely on the radio cricket commentator to paint the picture of a match for them. Many of them follow the placings and movements of fielders on a braille pattern of a cricket field. Some, like our special friend Mike Howell up at Old Trafford, actually come to the Tests, and listen in to our commentaries. They like to feel that they are part of the crowd and enjoy absorbing the excitement and atmosphere of everything happening at the ground.

Most of you will know that on every Saturday of a Test Match, in addition to 'A View from the Boundary', we make an appeal on behalf of the Primary Club. The qualification to join is simple. Whatever sex or age you are, or in whatever class of cricket, if you have ever been out first ball (except for a run-out) you are qualified to join. All you have to do is to send £10 to: Mike Thomas, P.O. Box 111, Bromley, Kent. He will then send you a tie and membership certificate. If you are a lady there are brooches instead of ties, and if you are feeling extra generous, you can send £15 instead of £10, and you will get *two* ties. The money received goes mostly to the Dorton School for the Blind at Sevenoaks. Originally it went towards their cricket only. But as more and more members joined, the money is now used on a broader basis, especially for sport. As an example, a perfectly equipped gymnasium has been built as the result of the generosity of 'first ballers'.

Some of the money is also distributed to the various blind cricket clubs round the country. I happen to be President of one of these clubs called Metro, a sports and social club for the visually handicapped. They play cricket and have given exhibitions of how to play blind cricket at the Oval and Lord's. They have also been the National Champions.

You can imagine therefore how pleased I was to receive a letter from a lady in Stow-on-the-Wold telling me that the world-famous blind pianist George Shearing came and lived there every summer, which he spent listening to *Test Match Special*. We immediately contacted him in New York and invited him to the first of the two Lord's Tests in 1990. MCC gave special permission for his wife, Elly, to accompany him up to our box in the pavilion—a privilege only those ladies who *work* in the pavilion enjoy.

I had met him just once, 44 years before

during a broadcast from a restaurant off Bond Street. I had forgotten what a wonderful sense of humour he possessed and from the moment he entered the box he had us all laughing. Two years later I went at *his* invitation, to hear him in a concert at the Festival Hall. He gave a marvellous performance and I was fascinated to watch his fingers moving swiftly across the keyboard, hitting all the right notes, none of which, of course, he could see. He is one of the happiest men I have ever met.

LORD'S, 23 JUNE 1990

BRIAN JOHNSTON Are you a jazz pianist, classical pianist, or just a pianist?

GEORGE SHEARING I'm a pianist who happens to play jazz. I have said this quite frequently. I'm also a pianist who happens to be blind, as opposed to a blind pianist. I may get blind when my work is done, but not before.

BRIAN We heard of your enthusiasm for cricket from, I think, a lady down in Stow-on-the-Wold, where you come every summer. You live in America now.

GEORGE Yes, we've lived in New York for

almost twelve years and we lived in California before then. What do you think about the retention of my accent? Is there much?

BRIAN There's a little tingle of American, but mostly it's the good old basic English. And it is pretty basic—it's Battersea, isn't it?

GEORGE It is. Until I was sixteen I was very much a Cockney and I think the thing that got me out of being a Cockney was when I was doing some broadcasts for the BBC and the announcer came on and said (very properly), 'For the next fifteen minutes you will be hearing the music of George Shearing.' I played the first medley and said, 'Good mornin'' everybody. We just played the medley of commercial popular numbers includin' "Tears on my Pillow", "Let Me Whisper I Love You", "Magyar Melody" and "Jeepers Creepers".' And the announcer came back after the show to say, 'For the last fifteen minutes you have been hearing the music of George Shearing.' Fortunately I had some good ears and I was able to dispense with the largest part of my Cockney accent.

I was in a residential school between the ages of twelve and sixteen—and I'm going to be 71 this August. In this school we played cricket. Now you can imagine blind people playing cricket. First of all we played in the gymnasium. We played with a rather large balloon-type ball with a bell in it and all the bowling was underhand, of course, and this ball would bounce along the gymnasium floor. The wicket was two large blocks of wood, perhaps fifteen or sixteen inches long, bolted together with a heavy nut and bolt on each end. Sandwiched in between was a piece of plywood, so that we could hear this ball when it hit the wicket. You'd know very well you were out if that happened.

BRIAN No disputing with the umpire.

GEORGE Dickie Bird would have no problems.

Now, if you hit the side wall it was one run; if you hit the end wall of the gymnasium it was two runs; if you hit the end wall without a bounce it was four; if you hit the ceiling at the other end it was six and if you hit the overmantel it was three weeks' suspension.

BRIAN Much the same rules for indoor cricket today. But—born blind—how do you picture a cricket ball or a cricket bat?

GEORGE When I was a kid I used to go out in the street and play cricket with sighted people. And my little nephew would hold the bat with me and he would indicate when he was going to swing it. We actually did make many contacts with the bat on the ball—a regular cricket bat and ball.

BRIAN What was your father? Was he a musician?

GEORGE No, Daddy was a coalman. He would deliver coal.

BRIAN With a horse and cart?

GEORGE Yes. I often wondered if he shouldn't put on his cart: 'COAL A LA CART OR CUL DE SACK'.

BRIAN Not a bad gag. Now, did he start you on music? How did you get into that?

GEORGE I'm the youngest of a family of nine. There were no musicians in the family at all, so I imagine that in a previous life I was Mozart's guide dog. I don't really know how it started.

BRIAN Can we have a look at your fingers? I'm always interested in the fingers of guitarists and pianists. Yours are fairly delicate. They're straight. They haven't been broken by a cricket ball. So when did you first feel the touch of a piano and decide that was what you wanted to do?

GEORGE Before actually trying to make music as a pianist, I would shy bottles out of the second-storey window and hear them hit the street and they would have quite musical sounds. I had quite good taste, because I would use milk bottles for classical music and beer bottles for jazz.

BRIAN I wouldn't talk too loud, because the police have probably got all the records. They've been looking for the chap who did that.

GEORGE I first put my hands on a piano, I

think, when I was three years of age. I was listening to the old crystal set. It was stuff like the Roy Fox band. Then I would go over to the piano and pick out the tune that I had just heard.

BRIAN Is there such a thing as Braille music?

GEORGE Very much so. In fact I've learnt a number of concertos in Braille and played them with many symphony orchestras in the United States. I have given that up because I'm a little afraid of memory lapse. I had one thirty-bar memory lapse, I remember, when I was playing with the Buffalo Symphony and my wife noticed that I was leaning towards the orchestra. Being, of course, a musician who plays jazz, on hearing the chords of the orchestra, I could immediately improvise in the style of Mozart until my mind decided to behave once again and go back to the score.

BRIAN So you can do it from Braille, but basically you're an ear pianist.

GEORGE Yes, very much. You see, if you were to do anything short of sitting on the piano, I could probably hear what you were playing. If you played a ten-note chord, I could probably hear.

BRIAN If I sat on it it would probably be a twenty-note chord.

GEORGE Well, I didn't say that.

BRIAN George, do you remember when we

first met?

GEORGE   Yes, it was in Fisher's restaurant in about 1946, when we were with the Frank Weir band.

BRIAN   We did a *Saturday Night Out* when I first joined the BBC. I joined in January and this must have been about April 1946. And I was amazed then as I talked to you and I asked how you were getting home. You said, 'Oh, I've come by tube, I shall be going home by tube.'

GEORGE   And I used to do it without the aid of a cane or a dog or anything else. We've had a man in the United States who used to do that. His name was Doctor Spanner and you could prove that he did it, because he had all kinds of bruises all over his body where he'd got into various accidents. They used to refer to him as 'the Scar-Spangled Spanner'.

BRIAN   But did you tap your way along Bond Street to the tube station?

GEORGE   When I started to use a cane I did. One time during World War Two I remember somebody said to me, 'Would you see me across the road?' And I took his arm and saw him across the road. It's the only case I've heard of the blind leading the blind.

BRIAN   Do you still walk around on your own if you know the district?

GEORGE   Not very much. One tends to lose one's nerve a little bit when you pass 65, I think.

BRIAN   Oh, get away! Describe for me what you think you're looking out at here.

GEORGE   Well, we are probably at one end of the cricket field and are we looking down the length of the pitch?

BRIAN   Yes.

GEORGE   I have light and dark, but that's all I have. Sitting in this box, of course, it's an interesting aspect of controlled acoustics and wonderful daylight and fresh air coming in through open windows. As a matter of fact I wouldn't mind buying a lifetime ticket here.

BRIAN   Well, you'd be most welcome. When we say that the umpire's wearing a white coat or the batsman plays a stroke, can you figure what that means?

GEORGE   No. Two things that a born-blind man would have difficulty with are colour and perspective. When you think about it, you can be satisfied that you're looking at a table on a flat piece of paper, although it obviously has cubic capacity. And I suppose my education and my instruction gives me the information that perhaps you draw two legs shorter than the other two and something about the way the light gets it. I have no conception at all of colours. In fact, once when I got a cab in the mid-town area of Chicago, I was to meet the Count Basie band on the South Side. They were all staying at a hotel mostly frequented by black

110

people at that time and I said to the cab driver, 'Could you take me to the South Central Hotel?' And he said, 'Do you know that's a coloured hotel?' I said, 'Really? What colour is it?' And when we got there I gave him a tip about twice the size one would normally do, to make up for his ignorance, got into the bus with the Basie band and took off and hoped that he was duly embarrassed.

BRIAN   Does green grass mean anything to you?

GEORGE   Oh, yes. What a lovely smell when it's freshly mowed and when it's been watered. It means a great deal to me. But I suppose if you want colour description, I would say that blue would be something peaceful, red would be something perhaps angry and green—I don't know.

BRIAN   Well, it's something very pleasant to look at, if you have a nice green cricket field.
    You've lived in America a long time—have you always liked cricket?

GEORGE   I've always been very fond of cricket, but, as you can imagine, being in America, one has had a great many years *in absentia*, which always makes me sad and I can't wait to get over here and render my wife a cricket widow.

BRIAN   How much do you come over now?

GEORGE   Three months a year and my aim is to make it six months a year.

111

BRIAN   You go to the Cotswolds and do you sit and listen to the Test Matches?

GEORGE   Oh, yes, of course I do. As a matter of fact, we may catch the three-thirty this afternoon, so that by five I can be in my deck chair in the garden listening to the rest of the afternoon's play. And incidentally, I think you're a very logical and wonderful follow-on from Howard Marshall.

BRIAN   Did you hear him?

GEORGE   Oh, many times.

BRIAN   Did you hear him describe Len Hutton's famous innings at the Oval—the 364?

GEORGE   Yes. I used to listen to him on the first radios I had in the thirties.

BRIAN   He was lovely to listen to. He could take his place here and show us up. In other sports, commentators of that vintage would be old-fashioned, but he would be absolutely perfect.

Are you a good impersonator? Can you pick up people's voices?

GEORGE   I used to do Norman Long monologues on my show.

BRIAN   'A   song,   a   smile   and   a piano'—Norman Long.

GEORGE   (*in character*)

I've saved up all the year for this
And here it is, no kid.
This here Irish Sweepstake ticket

And it cost me half a quid.
Not much of it to look at,
Bit expensive like, of course,
But if I draws a winner,
Gor, lumme, if I even draws a horse,
The quids, just think about them,
Thousands of them, lovely notes
Not greasy—nice and new.
I'll take me wife and family
Down to Margate by the sea.
Cockles, rock and winkles,
Shrimps and strawberries for tea.
A-sitting in your deckchairs,
With your conscience clear and sound,
A-smiling at the bloke and saying,
'Can you change a pound?'
Instead of hopping out of them
Each time the bloke comes round.
Thirty thousand quid!

BRIAN   That's marvellous. Did you get all
that from memory, or did you used to write
it down?

GEORGE   No, I never wrote it down. I
listened to it enough until I remembered it
and I've never forgotten it since 1935 or '36
when I first heard it, any more than I've
forgotten the geographical version of the
Lord's prayer.

BRIAN   Which is what?

GEORGE

How far is the White Hart from Hendon?

Harrow Road be thy name.

Thy Kingston come, Thy Wimbledon
In Erith as it is in Devon.

Give us this Bray our Maidenhead
And forgive us our Westminsters,

As we forgive those who Westminster against us.

And lead us not into Thames Ditton,
But deliver us from Yeovil [or from the Oval if you prefer]

For Thine is the Kingston and the Purley and

the Crawley

For Iver and Iver,

Crouch End.

BRIAN Have you ever done stand-up comedy?

GEORGE I'm far too lazy to do stand-up comedy. I sit down at the piano because I have embraced the philosophy for lo(!) these many years, 'Why should any man work when he has the health and strength to lie in bed?'

BRIAN You sit down at the piano. You had a quintet for many years which was famous. Did you enjoy playing with people, or do you prefer to be solo?

GEORGE Well, I enjoyed it for 29 years. I've

now pared down to just bass and piano, because I can address myself to being a more complete pianist with a much greater degree of freedom every night to create what comes into mind—obviously restricted by the chords of the particular tune that I happen to be playing.

BRIAN Now, in addition to playing, you are a composer. How many hits have you composed?

GEORGE Oh, I can play you a medley of my hit in two minutes. It's called 'Lullaby of Birdland'. I've composed about 99 other compositions which have gone from relative obscurity to total oblivion.

BRIAN But what do people want? When they see you they say, 'Come on, George, play ...' What?

GEORGE They still want 'September in the Rain', which was one of the quintet's most famous numbers. We did 90,000 copies of that. It was a 78 when it started.

BRIAN Now, 'Lullaby of Birdland'—I always thought that was a lovely lullaby of a little wood with the birds twittering, but Birdland wasn't actually that, was it?

GEORGE Birdland actually was a club in New York dedicated to Charlie Parker, who was nicknamed 'the Bird' and I've played Birdland many times. It was a little basement kind of dive.

BRIAN We have thousands of blind

115

listeners. Any word for them about cricket and what it's meant to you?

GEORGE   I hope they enjoy cricket as much as I do, because I really love it. Incidentally the Royal National Institute for the Blind put out the cricket fixtures in Braille.

BRIAN   If I was to ask you to sing or hum your favourite tune to finish, what would it be?

GEORGE   It would be almost anything of Cole Porter or Jerome Kern. One thing that comes to mind is:

> Whenever skies look grey to me
> And trouble begins to brew;
> Whenever the winter wind becomes too
>   strong,
> I concentrate on you—Graham Gooch
> I concentrate on you—Richard Hadlee.

THE RT. HON. JOHN MAJOR

At almost every Test Match from 1988 onwards, John Major has been a regular visitor to the *TMS* commentary box. It was always on a Friday and he was usually accompanied by his cricket-loving friend Robert Atkins, who later was to become Sports Minister. He would stay about half an hour and took an interest in all that was going on in the box. He also showed his expert knowledge on all aspects of cricket—tactics, techniques, records and so on. In fact, after our talk together on the air, he said he had hoped that I would have asked him what he thought of the modern game and what changes he would like to make in its laws and playing regulations. (This was in 1990, so perhaps it was a gentle hint that he would like to do another 'View from the Boundary'!)

When he first came to visit us he was Chief Secretary to HM Treasury, then had a brief spell as Foreign Secretary and by the summer of 1990 he was Chancellor of the Exchequer. Since he became Prime Minister at the end of November, 1990, his visits to our box have become rarer. This is partly due to his crowded programme of duties, and also to security, especially at grounds like Old Trafford where he has to walk round the ground to get to our box. In 1992, his duties were particularly arduous as he had a six-month session as President of the European Community. But he did find time to do a short interview at Lord's in which I chided him for allowing European affairs to interfere with cricket, and another by telephone to the Oval while he was at the Barcelona Olympic Games.

Cricket has been lucky to have a number of cricket-loving Prime Ministers—Stanley Baldwin, a member of MCC, Clement Attlee, Alec Douglas-Home (he played twice for Middlesex), Ted Heath (a keen Kent supporter who gave a splendid reception at No. 10 for Ray Illingworth's victorious team on their return from Australia in 1971) and now John Major.

I have one happy memory of John Major off-duty in 1992. Paul Getty opened his lovely cricket ground on his estate of Wormsley on the Buckinghamshire/Oxfordshire border. The opening match was Paul Getty's XI against MCC, which the Queen Mother and John Major attended. He spent a large part of the day bowling to a number of boys aged from four to ten behind the pavilion. If ever a man looked happy he did.

I'm not sure whether he bowled any of them out with his slow medium deliveries, but it did show what a great relaxation cricket can be, away from the stresses and responsibilities of a Prime Minister.

LORD'S, 28 JULY 1990

BRIAN JOHNSTON When did your interest in cricket start? You were born in Merton, so you were qualified for Surrey.

JOHN MAJOR I was qualified for Surrey in everything except talent. It really started when my family moved to Brixton and I was about ten. I was within walking distance of the Oval and that was at the time Surrey were beating everyone, generally within two days—that marvellous team that won the championship from '52 to '58 inclusive. It was, I think, probably the best county side I ever expect to see. They were truly magnificent and I watched them whenever I could.

BRIAN Where did you sit at the Oval, under the gasometer?

JOHN No, I sat on the other side. I sat at square leg with the batsman at the pavilion end, in the popular seats there and by pure habit I used to go there for years after as well.

BRIAN   What chances did you yourself get of playing cricket? Were you coached?

JOHN   I played a bit at school. We had quite a good cricket team at school. I played for them and I played a bit of cricket after school as well. I played a bit in Nigeria when I first went there at about twenty to do some banking. But my cricketing days came to an end after a motor car accident in Nigeria when I was twenty or so and I haven't played since.

(This interview came before the 1991 meeting of Commonwealth Prime Ministers in Zimbabwe when Mr Major opened the batting with the then Australian Prime Minister, Bob Hawke, in a match to mark the occasion. Ed.)

BRIAN   So we were robbed of—what? A fast bowler, or what would England have had if you'd been fit?

JOHN   You were robbed of an extremely mediocre medium-paced bowler.

BRIAN   Banking in Nigeria sounds an interesting job.

JOHN   Yes, it was. It was certainly that. The greatest enthusiasm that most of the people had there was for the weekly cricket match. They had their priorities absolutely right.

BRIAN   It does happen all round the world. So when you watched that Surrey side, were there any special favourites you picked out? Was it the bowlers you liked—Bedser, Laker or Lock?

120

JOHN   Oh, they were tremendous. It was such a superb team and they were so varied. I always thought Alec Bedser bowling was rather like a galleon in full sail coming up to the wicket. Last evening, Brian Rix said to me that he'd been batting a few years ago against Alec Bedser in a charity match and he'd said to Alec, 'Let me have an easy one to get off the mark.' And he said Alec couldn't do it. He couldn't bowl the bad ball. And I can well believe it. But the rest of the team were superb. I used to time, with an old stopwatch I had, how long it took the ball from leaving Peter May's bat to hitting the boundary. It wasn't long.

BRIAN   Ah, those famous on-drives.

JOHN   And I think that Tony Lock was the most aggressive-looking bowler I ever saw—and fielder.

BRIAN   And a little lesson in leadership, too, because old Stewy Surridge was a tremendous leader. He was a very forceful leader, too.

JOHN   He was. I met Stuart Surridge for the first time about six weeks ago. It was a very great thrill. I remember thinking as a boy, when I watched him standing there, round the wicket, where he fielded absolutely magnificently, that he was one of the few men I've ever seen who could scratch his toes while standing upright. He had these amazingly long arms and he just caught

121

everything—truly wonderful.
(Sadly, Stuart Surridge died in 1992 at the age of 74. Ed.)

BRIAN   Very brave he was, but then they all were—Micky Stewart and Locky walking in when he was fielding at backward short leg, which not many short legs do.

JOHN   Some of Lock's catches are still unbelievable even in retrospect. You just didn't know how he got there and how he held it.

BRIAN   But when did you see your first Test Match? Do you remember that?

JOHN   Well, I remember the first Test Match I listened to seriously. It was an Indian Test Match and it was in 1952 when India were nought for four in the second innings.

BRIAN   We had a certain gentleman—Fred Trueman—in here just now, who was not unconcerned with that.

JOHN   He took three of the four wickets. It was an astonishing scorecard.

BRIAN   But have you been able to go to Test Matches much?

JOHN   I've been to quite a few—a good deal fewer than I would wish to have gone to, but, yes, I've been to quite a few over the years. I saw a bit of the last Test Match in 1953 when the Ashes came back and I saw some of the '56 series.

BRIAN   I wonder, when you have all these

conferences, are you ever brought in notes with the latest score?

JOHN Certainly in the period I was Chief Secretary and we had great negotiations with colleagues about spending matters, the meetings did used to break up for critical parts of the Test Match, to watch it. My then secretary, who was a Surrey member and a fanatical cricketer, used to send in notes to say the Test Match had reached a critical stage and we used to break up and watch it. Nigel Lawson is also a great cricket supporter—a great Leicestershire fan—and we used to sit there, with Nigel in the chair, his fellow ministers, lots of extremely important mandarins and others at the other side of the table and a piece of paper would come in that would be passed gravely round the table. It was the Test score, it wasn't the markets, I promise you.

BRIAN Did you just nod as though it was important financial news?

JOHN Well, over the last couple of years, some of it was very grave.

BRIAN Are quite a few members of the Cabinet keen followers?

JOHN The best cricket player in the Cabinet is probably Tom King. He is a good cricketer.

BRIAN He also keeps wicket, I think.

JOHN He keeps wicket as well. Peter Brooke is a walking Wisden and knows a great deal about cricket.

BRIAN We could put him against the Bearded Wonder and he'd stump him, d'you think?

(The Bearded Wonder is, of course, Bill Frindall. Ed.)

JOHN Well, I think as a non-gambling man, I might put my money on the Bearded Wonder, but not by much. Peter Brooke knows a great deal about it and there are a number of others.

BRIAN I suppose, because you were injured, you haven't been able to play for the Lords and Commons.

JOHN No, I'm afraid that motor accident ended my playing days. I wouldn't run too well now, otherwise I would love to play.

BRIAN They play some very good cricket. It mingles up the parties, too. They don't seem to bother about the politics.

JOHN Indeed not. Bob Cryer, the Labour MP for one of the Bradford seats, is a very fine left-arm slow bowler. There are some good cricketers right across the Commons.

BRIAN What's the first thing you read in the papers in the morning?

JOHN I do read the sports pages every day. I tend to read Matthew Engel when he writes cricket. That is the first thing I turn to in that particular newspaper.

(Matthew Engel was appointed editor of Wisden in 1992. Ed.)

I much miss the fact that Jim Swanton doesn't write quite as regularly as once he did. I thought he was supremely good and I much enjoy reading Tony Lewis. But I do turn to the sports pages at an early stage in the morning.

BRIAN Are you great on the literature of cricket? Have you got a big library of cricket books?

JOHN Well, quite big, yes. I do read a lot of cricket. I've been trying to get hold of a book on cricket that Richard Daft wrote a long time ago—way back in the 1870s or 1880s. Richard Daft's great grandson, incidentally, is the Cabinet Secretary, Robin Butler—another fine cricketer. The Civil Service has some extremely good cricketers. But I haven't been able to find that book in old bookshops. Robert Atkins has a copy, which he jealously guards and lends to me occasionally.

(As a result of this broadcast, Mr Major received a copy of the Richard Daft book. Ed.)

BRIAN What other great cricket writers in the newspapers do you remember especially?

JOHN In the evening papers, when one used to go out and see how Surrey were doing and whether the game would go into a third day, I remember reading E. M. Wellings a lot.

BRIAN He wrote a lot of very good sense—and played for Surrey, too.

JOHN And of course, in terms of literature,

like everybody, I've read a lot of Cardus.

BRIAN Which is absolutely marvellous stuff. He and Arlott and Swanton—and Robertson Glasgow—did you ever read him?

JOHN I've not read a lot of him.

BRIAN Well, if you can get any of his little vignettes about players, they were absolutely brilliant. He was the chap who said, 'Hammond, like a ship in full sail', which was a perfect description of Hammond going to the wicket.

JOHN I wish I'd seen him bat, too.

BRIAN But I suppose you don't get a lot of time to read, do you?

JOHN Well, I do, actually. Whatever time I go to bed, I tend to pick up a book for half an hour or 45 minutes, just to wash away the rest of the day, and it is often a cricket book.

BRIAN I hope that doesn't send you to sleep.

JOHN Well I go to sleep, but it's not the book.

BRIAN Young James, your son, is he a good cricketer?

JOHN He's a better footballer and for the reason that there isn't as much cricket at schools as there ought to be. The point about cricket in schools is that it takes such a long time-span. That's the real difficulty and whereas I think the staff are willingly prepared to give up an afternoon for a football match to get the pupils there, play the game and get them back, it is a good deal longer for a cricket match.

BRIAN   Are you a quick learner? I mean you had to switch suddenly to the Foreign Office. How did you brief yourself in that short time, because you appeared terribly knowledgeable when you went to conferences immediately afterwards.

JOHN   Well, you're very kind to say so. You read a lot and hopefully recall. It's really a problem of total immersion. It's the same in cricket in many ways. I'm sorry to name-drop, but I bumped into Arthur Morris today—a very great player—and he remembered hitting Wilf Wooller for four fours off the first four balls of a game down in Glamorgan. And I said, 'That was a bit extravagant.' And he said, 'Not as extravagant as the field that had been set,' which he then described to me. So I think these things just stick in the mind. He, 40 years on, remembers the field placing.

BRIAN   If you ask Fred Trueman about any of the wickets he took or the innings he played, he'd tell you exactly. He's got a marvellous memory.

JOHN   Yes, it's a great gift.

BRIAN   Are you great on music?

JOHN   I like music very much and I go whenever I can, which isn't as often as I would wish, with Norma. She's forgotten more about music than I'll ever know.

BRIAN   And besides cricket, any particular hobby?

JOHN   Well, I read a lot; I'm very fond of the theatre; I go and watch a fair bit of football and athletics if I can—most sport.

BRIAN   John Major, thank you very much. You're a cricket fanatic and a man after our own hearts and I hope you'll continue to listen to us.

JOHN   Brian, I will. I wouldn't miss it for the world.